American Sign Language for Beginners

4-Week Comprehensive ASL Guide
to Learn Sign Language.
Basic Signs, Expressions & Simple Techniques
for Everyday Communication

American Sign Language for Beginners

CONTENT

INTRODUCTION.. 5

WEEK I: AMERICAN SIGN LANGUAGE (ASL)
FUNDAMENTALS.. 8

Lesson 1: The Importance of Learning ASL 8

Lesson 2: History and development of ASL 10

Lesson 3: Facial Expressions and Body Language 13

Lesson 4: ASL Alphabet Basics 24

Lesson 5: The Basic Signing Parameters 27

WEEK II: ESSENTIAL SKILLS.. 31

Lesson 6: Pronouns in ASL.. 31

Lesson 7: Number Basic... 41

Lesson 8: Days of the Week. Tenses and Time............................... 55

Lesson 9: Most Common Signs 60

Lesson 10: Sentence structure. Questions & Answers.................... 63

WEEK III: DAY-TO-DAY USE 67

Lesson 11: Colors, Shapes, and Descriptors 67

Lesson 12: Family and Friends 71

Lesson 13: Food and drink... 76

Lesson 14: Verbs in ASL 82

Lesson 15: Most Common phrases 88

WEEK IV: COMMUNICATION SKILLS IMPROVEMENT
.... 93

Lesson 16: Medical and Emergency Signs 93

Lesson 17: ASL for Parents and Guardians.................................... 99

Lesson 18: More important communication topics 102

Lesson 19: Expansion Techniques 118

Lesson 20: Top Digital Resources for Learning ASL 120

BONUS: BILINGUALISM - ASL AND ENGLISH 124

CONCLUSION 129

Introduction

Welcome to the world of American Sign Language (ASL)! Whether you're a beginner eager to embark on a new language journey or someone seeking to enhance their communication skills, this book is your comprehensive guide to ASL. In this introductory chapter, we'll set the stage for your ASL adventure and provide an overview of what you can expect to learn.

Why ASL Matters

ASL is more than just a language; it's a bridge to a vibrant and diverse community. Understanding and using ASL can open doors to meaningful connections, both with Deaf individuals and within the broader Deaf culture. Learning ASL is not just about acquiring a new skill; it's about fostering inclusivity, breaking down communication barriers, and celebrating linguistic diversity.

What Will You Learn?

This book is designed to take you from the basics of ASL to a level of proficiency where you can engage in meaningful conversations, express yourself fluently, and navigate various aspects of Deaf culture. Here's an overview of what you'll learn throughout the chapters:

ASL Fundamentals: Start with the building blocks of ASL, including the manual alphabet, numbers, and essential signs. You'll gain a solid foundation in the language's structure and grammar.

Everyday Communication: Explore everyday communication topics such as greetings, introductions, and common phrases. Practice your conversational skills and learn how to express yourself in various social situations.

Family and Friends: Dive into the world of relationships and learn signs for family members, friends, and important life events. Discover how ASL strengthens bonds and enables heartfelt communication.

Food and Drink: Delve into the delicious world of food and beverages. Master the signs for various foods, drinks, and meal-related phrases, allowing you to engage in culinary conversations.

Verbs in ASL: Understand the unique structure of ASL verbs, from action verbs to directional verbs. Learn how to convey actions and activities effectively.

Colors, Shapes, and Descriptors: Expand your descriptive vocabulary by learning signs for colors, shapes, and descriptive adjectives. Enhance your ability to express details and attributes.

Medical and Emergency Signs: Equip yourself with essential signs related to medical situations and emergencies. Learn to communicate effectively in critical moments.

ASL for Parents and Guardians: Discover phrases and signs designed for parents and guardians, enabling you to communicate with children effectively and lovingly.

More Important Communication Topics: Explore a wide range of topics, from expressing emotions and discussing hobbies to addressing cultural awareness and navigating various aspects of life.

Expansion Techniques: Enhance your signing skills by exploring techniques to expand your ASL vocabulary and fluency.

Top Digital Resources for Learning ASL: Discover valuable online resources and tools to support your ASL learning journey.

Your ASL Journey Begins

Your journey into the world of ASL is an exciting and transformative experience. Along the way, you'll not only acquire a new language but also gain cultural insights, connect with others, and contribute to a more inclusive society. Whether you're learning ASL for personal growth, professional development, or to foster meaningful relationships, your dedication to this journey is commendable.

Let's dive into the rich and expressive language of ASL. The adventure begins now, and by the end of this book, you'll have the tools and knowledge to communicate confidently and respectfully in ASL. So, let's start!

Week I: American Sign Language (ASL) Fundamentals

Lesson 1: The Importance of Learning ASL

In today's interconnected world, communication is key to building relationships, sharing ideas, and fostering understanding among diverse groups. American Sign Language (ASL) offers a unique and vital means of communication, particularly for the Deaf and hard of hearing community. Learning ASL is not just about acquiring a new language; it's about embracing an entire culture, opening doors to new experiences, and breaking down barriers that have long stood between the hearing and the Deaf communities.

ASL has a rich history that is deeply entwined with the Deaf community. Its origins can be traced back to the early 19th century, merging French Sign Language with existing sign systems in the United States. Over the years, ASL has evolved, shaped by the culture and experiences of its users.

The journey of ASL from a marginalized form of communication to an officially recognized language highlights significant social progress. Legal and educational reforms over the years have underscored the importance of ASL in ensuring equal opportunities and access for the Deaf community.

ASL is more than a language; it is a cornerstone of Deaf culture. It embodies a rich tapestry of traditions, stories, and values passed down through generations. For many Deaf individuals, ASL is not just a means of communication but a source of identity and pride.

Understanding ASL offers insights into Deaf culture, fostering a deeper appreciation of its history, art, and community dynamics. This cultural immersion enhances one's perspective on diversity and inclusivity.

Learning ASL has numerous benefits, both personal and societal. On a personal level, it stimulates cognitive development, enhances creativity, and opens up a new dimension of non-verbal communication skills. Professionally, it can lead to career opportunities in fields like education, interpretation, social work, and more.

On a broader scale, knowing ASL bridges the gap between the Deaf and hearing communities. It promotes inclusivity, understanding, and respect. In settings like education, healthcare, and public services, ASL proficiency can make a significant difference in the quality of service and accessibility.

Incorporating ASL into daily life enriches interactions and experiences. Whether it's communicating with a Deaf colleague, engaging in community events, or enjoying ASL literature and art, the language offers a new lens through which to view the world.

The importance of learning ASL cannot be overstated. It's a journey into a vibrant culture, a tool for personal and professional growth, and a step towards a more inclusive society. By embracing ASL, we not only learn a new language but also become part of a larger, diverse community united by the power of communication.

Lesson 2: History and development of ASL

Gallaudet's meeting with Laurent Clerc in France was a pivotal moment in the history of American Sign Language. Clerc, who was a successful Deaf teacher at the Royal Institution for the Deaf in Paris, used French Sign Language (LSF) effectively in his teachings. Inspired by Clerc's methods and the potential of sign language in education, Gallaudet invited him to America to help establish a school for the Deaf.

In 1817, Gallaudet and Clerc co-founded the American School for the Deaf in Hartford, Connecticut. This institution became the cornerstone for Deaf education in the United States. The blend of LSF and the native sign languages used by American Deaf students resulted in a rich, evolving language. This language, which we now know as American Sign Language, was not a direct copy of LSF but rather a unique creation that emerged from this fertile cross-cultural exchange.

The establishment of the American School for the Deaf marked the beginning of an era where ASL started to flourish. The language spread as Deaf students from different parts of the United States came to study at the school and then returned to their homes, taking ASL with them. This period saw the growth of a distinct Deaf community in America, unified by a common language. As the language spread, it continued to evolve, incorporating elements from the various home sign systems that students brought with them.

Deaf teachers, like Clerc, played a crucial role in the propagation and development of ASL. They were instrumental in shaping the language, as their natural use of signs provided a robust model for their students. The early Deaf teachers' community also contributed significantly to the development of a standardized form of ASL, which facilitated more consistent communication among the widespread Deaf communities.

Despite the growing use of ASL, the late 19th and early 20th centuries saw significant challenges. The Milan Conference of 1880, which advocated for oralism, led to a widespread suppression of sign language in Deaf education. However, ASL persisted in Deaf communities, passed down through generations in social settings and Deaf clubs. This resilience under adversity highlighted the importance of ASL as not just a means of communication, but as a vital component of Deaf identity and culture.

The Milan Conference of 1880

The outcomes of the Milan Conference of 1880 had far-reaching consequences for the Deaf community. The endorsement of oralism over manualism not only led to the widespread banning of sign language in educational settings but also propagated a negative view of sign languages in general. This shift significantly impacted the Deaf community, as ASL and other sign languages were seen as inferior to spoken languages, and their use was actively discouraged.

This period of decline in ASL usage was marked by a struggle for Deaf individuals to maintain their cultural identity. In the face of these adversities, however, Deaf communities found ways to preserve their language. Secretly, and in private settings, ASL continued to be a vital means of communication. These underground practices played a crucial role in keeping ASL alive, passing it from generation to generation.

Despite the oppressive measures following the Milan Conference, the Deaf community demonstrated remarkable resilience. Deaf clubs and social gatherings became sanctuaries where ASL could be used freely. These spaces were not just about preserving a language; they were about maintaining a community and a culture that had been pushed to the margins of society.

In these environments, ASL evolved organically. Deaf individuals from various regions brought their unique signs and expressions, enriching the language. This period of underground development was critical in ensuring that ASL retained its vibrancy and complexity.

The true turning point came mid-20th century when the tide began to shift back in favor of ASL. The growing civil rights movement in the United States, which advocated for the rights of various marginalized groups, also positively impacted the Deaf community. There was a growing awareness and acceptance of the importance of cultural and linguistic diversity, and with it, a renewed interest in sign languages as legitimate forms of communication.

Lesson 3: Facial Expressions and Body Language

Facial expressions in ASL do more than just convey emotions; they are essential for grammatical purposes. For instance, the way one raises or furrows their eyebrows can change a statement into a question. Raised eyebrows often indicate a yes/no question, while furrowed brows are used for open-ended, or WH-questions (who, what, where, when, why). This distinction is crucial as it affects how the receiver interprets the sign's meaning.

Moreover, facial expressions can intensify or modify the meaning of a sign. A sign for 'happy' can be made more intense with an exaggerated smiling expression, indicating extreme happiness. Conversely, the same sign made with a neutral expression might convey a milder form of happiness. This flexibility allows signers to express a wide range of emotions and subtleties, making ASL a deeply expressive language.

Eye gaze, too, plays a significant role in ASL. Directional gaze can indicate the subject or object of a sentence, or even imply a location. For example, shifting one's gaze towards a particular direction while signing can indicate the location of the object being discussed. This non-verbal cue is crucial for providing spatial and referential context, which is vital in a visual language like ASL.

Lip movements, though often subtle, are also integral. Certain signs are accompanied by specific mouth shapes or movements, which can change the sign's meaning. For example, the sign for 'not yet' involves a specific mouth movement that is different from the sign for 'late', although the handshape and movement are similar. Mastering these nuances is vital for clear communication.

Facial expressions and body language in ASL are not only about conveying information; they also reflect cultural respect and understanding. The Deaf community places great importance on expressive communication, considering it a sign of engagement and respect in conversation. Thus, learning to use facial expressions effectively is not just a linguistic skill but also a way to show cultural sensitivity and build stronger connections within the Deaf community.

In conclusion, facial expressions in ASL are multifaceted tools that provide grammatical cues, emotional context, and cultural significance. Understanding and mastering them is key to becoming a proficient signer and an effective communicator in the world of ASL.

In addition to the raised and furrowed eyebrows for questions, other facial expressions play a pivotal role in conveying emotions and meanings in ASL. A crucial aspect is understanding the subtlety and variety of these expressions, as they can significantly alter the meaning of signs.

Happiness: A smiling face, often with eyes squinted slightly, is used to express joy or happiness. This expression can be used with a variety of signs to enhance the positive emotion being conveyed.

Sadness: To express sadness, the eyebrows are often drawn together, with the corners of the mouth turned down. The eyes may also appear softer or slightly teary, adding to the expression of sorrow.

Surprise: A surprised expression involves wide eyes and often a dropped jaw. This expression can accompany signs to indicate shock or unexpectedness.

Anger: Anger is shown through narrowed eyes, a furrowed brow, and often a tightened or closed mouth. This expression can intensify the severity of the emotion being signed.

Confusion: A confused expression may include a tilted head, a furrowed brow, and a slightly open mouth. This is particularly useful in ASL to indicate misunderstanding or the need for clarification.

Exercises to Practice Mirroring Expressions: Expression Imitation: Practice imitating the expressions described above in front of a mirror. Pay attention to the nuances of each emotion and try to replicate them as accurately as possible.

Expression Matching with Signs: Pair up common signs with the appropriate facial expressions. For example, practice signing "happy" with a joyful expression or "confused" with the corresponding confused facial expression.

Role-Playing Scenarios: Engage in role-playing exercises where you use ASL to communicate in different emotional contexts. For instance, have a conversation where you express surprise or happiness using both signs and facial expressions.

Video Recording and Analysis: Record yourself signing with different facial expressions. Review the video to see if the expressions are clear and appropriate for the signs used. This can help in self-assessment and improvement.

Group Practice Sessions: If possible, practice with other ASL learners or fluent signers. This can provide valuable feedback and the opportunity to observe and mimic a variety of expressions.

By regularly practicing these exercises, learners can develop a more intuitive and natural use of facial expressions, enhancing their overall ASL communication skills. Remember, facial expressions in ASL are not just about showing emotion; they are an integral part of conveying meaning and intent.

The use of the entire body in ASL is not just a supplement to hand signs; it is a core component of conveying accurate and nuanced messages. Understanding and mastering body language is essential for anyone learning ASL.

Posture: The posture of a signer can convey a variety of messages and emotions. For example, leaning forward slightly can indicate interest or intensity, while a relaxed, upright posture may convey a more casual or neutral tone. Slumped shoulders might suggest sadness or disinterest. Being mindful of posture helps in delivering the intended message more effectively.

Shoulder Movements: Shoulders are often used to emphasize certain signs or to express emotions. A quick shrug can indicate a question or uncertainty. Raising the shoulders can intensify a sign, adding emphasis to the message being conveyed.

Body Orientation: The direction in which the body is facing plays a significant role in ASL. Orienting the body towards the person you are communicating with shows engagement and respect. In contrast, turning away can indicate disengagement or the end of a conversation. Furthermore, shifting body orientation can be used to represent different characters in a story or conversation.

Use of Space: ASL uses the space around the signer effectively. For example, setting up a spatial area to the signer's left or right can represent different people in a conversation, and the signer can turn towards that space to address that person. This technique is particularly useful in storytelling or explaining scenarios with multiple characters.

Facial Expression and Body Language Coordination: It is crucial to coordinate facial expressions with body language. A mismatch between the two can lead to confusion or misinterpretation of the sign. For example, a sign for 'happy' with a smiling face should also have an open, relaxed body posture to convey the emotion effectively.

Recording and Self-Evaluation: Record your signing sessions and evaluate your use of body language. Look for consistency between your facial expressions, body movements, and the signs you are using.

Role-Playing: Engage in role-playing exercises with different scenarios. Practice changing your body orientation, posture, and shoulder movements to fit different roles or emotions.

Group Feedback: Practice signing in a group and give each other feedback on body language. This can provide diverse perspectives and help improve your skills.

Body Language Immersion: Observe fluent ASL users, especially in natural settings. Pay attention to how they use their body language in different contexts and try to incorporate similar movements into your practice.

By integrating effective body language with hand signs and facial expressions, an ASL user can communicate more dynamically and expressively. This holistic approach is what makes ASL a rich and deeply communicative language.

Non-Manual Signals (NMS) in ASL encompass various facial and bodily cues that are not made with the hands but are essential for conveying complete information and context. These signals include movements and expressions of the eyes, mouth, head, and even the torso.

Eye Movements and Expressions: The eyes play a significant role in ASL. For example, wide eyes can express surprise or intensity, while squinting can indicate skepticism or a question. Eye gaze is also used to indicate directional verbs or to show the object or subject of a sentence.

Mouth Movements and Shapes: Mouth movements in ASL are not random; they are an integral part of the grammar. Different mouth shapes can modify the meaning of signs. For instance, a pursed lip can indicate a medium distance, while a mouth opened wide can indicate something large or extensive.

Head Movements: Nodding or shaking the head in ASL is similar to their use in spoken language, indicating agreement or disagreement. Tilting the head can indicate interest, curiosity, or be used as a part of a question. Head movements can also be used for emphasis in ASL.

Facial Expressions: As mentioned earlier, facial expressions are key in ASL, but when discussed as NMS, they refer specifically to the use of expressions to convey grammatical information. For example, a raised eyebrow can turn a statement into a question.

Torso Movements: The movement or orientation of the torso can add emphasis or context to a sign. Leaning forward can indicate intensity or interest, while leaning back can show disinterest or distance.

Examples of NMS and Their Interpretations:

- **Yes/No Questions:** Raised eyebrows, slightly leaned forward body, and wide eyes.

WH-Questions (Who, What, Where, When, Why): Furrowed eyebrows, tilted head, and direct eye contact.

- **Topicalization (Highlighting a Topic):** Raised eyebrows and a slight forward tilt of the head when introducing a topic.

Negation: Shaking the head while signing can indicate negation or disagreement.

- **Rhetorical Questions:** Raised eyebrows with a tilted head, often with a sustained gaze, indicating that no answer is expected.

Exercises to Enhance NMS Skills

Mirror Practice: Use a mirror to practice various NMS, paying close attention to your facial expressions, eye movements, and head tilts.

Video Analysis: Watch videos of fluent ASL signers and take note of their use of NMS. Try to identify different NMS and their context.

Pair Practice: Work with a partner and practice signing sentences to each other, focusing on using appropriate NMS. Your partner can provide feedback on your use of NMS.

Imitation Exercises: Try to mimic the NMS used by experienced signers. This can help in understanding how these signals are used naturally in conversation.

Storytelling Practice: Create stories using ASL and make a conscious effort to include NMS. Storytelling can be a fun way to practice a variety of NMS in different contexts.

Integrating facial expressions and body language into ASL is crucial for effective communication. Here are some additional tips to help you incorporate these elements more naturally into your signing:

Start Simple: Begin with basic expressions and gestures. Practice using them with signs you are already comfortable with. This will help you get used to coordinating your expressions and signs.

Exaggerate at First: Initially, it might be helpful to exaggerate your facial expressions and body language. This can make it easier to become aware of your non-verbal cues and how they impact your signing.

Observe and Imitate Experienced Signers: Watching experienced ASL users can provide insights into how they integrate non-manual signals seamlessly. Try to mimic their style to enhance your own skills.

Get Feedback: If possible, seek feedback from experienced ASL users or instructors. They can provide valuable insights into how well your facial expressions and body language are integrating with your signs.

Slow Down: When practicing, take your time. Rushing through signs can make it difficult to incorporate facial expressions and body language effectively.

Practice in Context: Practice signing in different contexts and scenarios. For example, signing in a storytelling session can help you learn how to change expressions and body language as the story progresses.

Emotionally Connect with Your Signs: Try to feel the emotions that your signs are conveying. This emotional connection can make your expressions and body language more authentic.

Consistency is Key: Be consistent with your practice. Regular practice helps to develop muscle memory, making it easier to naturally integrate facial expressions and body language into your signing over time.

By following these tips and incorporating them into your daily practice, you'll be able to communicate more effectively and expressively in ASL. Remember, non-verbal aspects of ASL are just as important as the signs themselves, and mastering them is a significant step towards fluency.

Expression of Identity: In the Deaf community, ASL is more than a language; it's an integral part of their identity. The use of facial expressions and body language in ASL is a form of art and a way of life. These aspects provide a sense of belonging and pride among Deaf individuals.

Cultural Norms and Etiquette: In Deaf culture, maintaining eye contact during communication is considered respectful. It shows attentiveness and interest. Similarly, exaggerated facial expressions and body movements are not viewed as overly dramatic but as appropriate and necessary for clear communication.

Historical Context: Historically, Deaf individuals have faced communication barriers and societal exclusion. ASL, with its rich use of expressions and gestures, has been a powerful tool in overcoming these barriers, allowing the Deaf community to forge strong bonds and a unique cultural identity.

Storytelling Traditions: Storytelling in the Deaf community is a cherished tradition, where facial expressions and body language play a crucial role. These stories are not just entertainment; they're a means of preserving history, sharing experiences, and imparting moral lessons.

Education and Learning: In Deaf education, teachers use expressive ASL to engage and teach students. This approach is not just effective for language acquisition but also helps in the emotional and social development of Deaf children.

Cultural Respect: For ASL learners, understanding and correctly using facial expressions and body language is a sign of respect for Deaf culture. It shows a willingness to fully immerse in the language and appreciate the nuances of Deaf communication.

Bridging Cultures: Proficiency in ASL, including its non-verbal aspects, allows hearing individuals to bridge the gap between Deaf and hearing cultures. This fosters inclusivity, understanding, and respect.

The Artistic Aspect: In Deaf culture, ASL is often considered a visual art form. Poems, stories, and performances in ASL showcase the beauty and expressiveness of the language, celebrating its cultural significance.

Lesson 4: ASL Alphabet Basics

The manual alphabet in ASL is a direct representation of the English alphabet through unique handshapes. Each letter has a specific form that needs to be clearly articulated to avoid misunderstandings. In this section, we provide a comprehensive breakdown of each letter, emphasizing the intricacies of handshapes and positioning.

Letter A: Form a fist with the thumb positioned alongside the index finger. Ensure the thumb is visible from the viewer's perspective.

Letter B: Extend all fingers straight, keeping them together, and tuck the thumb across the palm under the fingers.

Letter C: Shape your hand to resemble a 'C'. Keep your fingers curved and the thumb in line with the fingers.

Letter D: Raise the index finger while forming a circle with the thumb and remaining fingers.

Letter E: Curl the fingertips down to the thumb, keeping the thumb positioned under the fingers.

Letter F: Touch the tip of your thumb to the tip of your index finger, creating a circle, and extend the remaining fingers.

Letter G: Extend the index and thumb fingers, positioning them to make a right angle. The rest of the fingers are curled.

Letter H: Similar to 'G', but both the index and middle fingers are extended, forming a parallel line.

Letter I: Extend the pinky finger, with the rest of the fingers curled into the palm and the thumb resting on the side.

Letter J: Make the 'I' handshape, and then move the pinky in a sweeping 'J' motion.

Letter K: Extend the index and middle fingers in a 'V' shape, and place the thumb in between, slightly touching the middle finger.

Letter L: Extend the thumb and index finger to form an 'L' shape, with the other fingers curled down.

Letter M: Tuck three fingers (index, middle, and ring) over the thumb, which is placed against the palm.

Letter N: Similar to 'M', but with only two fingers (index and middle) over the thumb.

Letter O: Make an 'O' shape by touching the fingertips to the thumb, forming a circle.

Letter P: Form a 'K' handshape and then rotate your hand so that your palm is facing outward.

Letter Q: Like 'G', but with the palm facing behind you, and the angle of the thumb and index finger pointing downwards.

Letter R: Cross your index finger over your middle finger, slightly bending both, and keep the other fingers curled.

Letter S: Make a fist with the thumb in front of the fingers, not tucked in.

Letter T: Tuck the thumb between the index and middle finger, near the top of the palm.

Letter U: Extend the index and middle fingers while keeping them together, and curl the other fingers into the palm.

Letter V: Extend the index and middle fingers away from each other to form a 'V', with the other fingers curled into the palm.

Letter W: Like 'V', but with the ring finger also extended, forming a wider shape.

Letter X: Extend the index finger and curl it slightly at the knuckle, with the other fingers curled into the palm.

Letter Y: Extend the thumb and pinky finger, keeping the other fingers curled into the palm.

Letter Z: Draw a 'Z' in the air with the index finger, or simply sign it as you would write it.

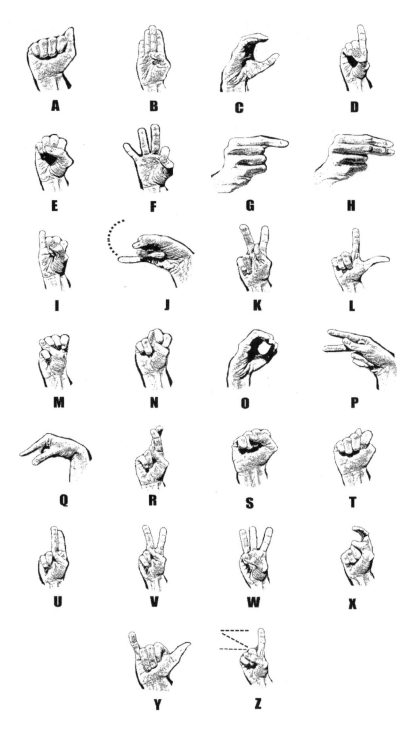

Lesson 5: The Basic Signing Parameters

The accuracy of hand position and orientation is paramount in ASL, as slight variations can lead to miscommunication. Here, we offer detailed guidance to ensure precise and clear hand positioning for each letter.

Palm Orientation: Most of the letters in the ASL alphabet are signed with the palm facing the viewer. However, some letters, like 'G' and 'H', require the palm to face sideways. Being mindful of palm orientation is crucial for the legibility of each letter.

Height and Placement: The standard position for signing the alphabet is in front of the torso, at about chest level. This placement ensures visibility and comfort. Holding your hand too high or too low can be straining and may hinder clear communication.

Steadiness and Control: Keep your hand steady while signing each letter. Avoid shaking or unnecessary movement, as this can distort the letter's shape and make it difficult to understand.

Relaxed Hand Posture: While precision is important, avoid tensing your hand muscles excessively. A relaxed hand is more fluid and can transition between letters more smoothly.

Finger Positioning: Pay close attention to the position of each finger. For example, in the letter 'E', the fingers need to be close to the thumb but not overly squeezed. Similarly, in 'K', the middle finger needs to be close to the thumb without touching it.

Consistency in Formation: Consistency in how you form each letter is key. Practice forming each letter the same way every time to build muscle memory and ensure your signing is easily understood.

Adjusting for Clarity: If someone doesn't understand a letter you've signed, try adjusting your hand position slightly. Sometimes a small change in angle or position can make a big difference in clarity.

Slow Down: When practicing, take it slow. Rushing through the alphabet can lead to sloppy handshapes and positions. Speed will naturally increase as you become more comfortable.

Smooth Transition: Practice transitioning smoothly between letters. Jerky or abrupt movements can make it difficult for the viewer to follow along. Aim for fluid motion from one letter to the next.

Bouncing and Pausing: A slight bounce or pause can be used to indicate the separation between words or syllables, especially in longer words. This helps in improving readability.

Consistent Orientation: Maintain a consistent orientation toward your audience. Avoid rotating your wrist or flipping your hand, as this can make your spelling difficult to read.

Eye Contact and Facial Expressions: Maintain eye contact with your audience while finger spelling. Using appropriate facial expressions can also provide contextual clues and enhance communication.

Double Letters: For words with double letters, slightly slide your hand to the side for the second letter or make a small bounce. This indicates that the letter is repeated.

Single Letter Practice: Start by practicing each letter of the alphabet individually. Focus on the correct handshape and positioning for each letter. Repeat until you can form each letter quickly and accurately.

Name Spelling: Practice spelling your name and the names of family members or friends. Names are often used in ASL conversations, so this practice can be particularly useful.

Timed Drills: Set a timer and see how many words you can finger spell correctly in a certain period. Start with a longer duration, like five minutes, and gradually decrease the time as you improve.

Reverse Reading: Record yourself finger spelling a list of words. Then, play the recording back and try to read what you spelled. This exercise helps in improving both spelling and reading skills.

Syllable Practice: Break down longer words into syllables and practice spelling them separately. Then, spell the whole word in sequence. This helps in managing more complex words.

Finger Spelling Games: Engage in finger spelling games, such as finger spelling bee, where you compete with others to spell words correctly. This can be both fun and educational.

Silent Practice: Practice finger spelling without voicing the letters. This reinforces the visual aspect of the language and helps you rely less on auditory cues.

Category Sorting: Choose a category (e.g., animals, foods, cities) and finger spell words that fit into that category. This helps in expanding your vocabulary while practicing finger spelling.

Sentence Spelling: Once comfortable with spelling words, start practicing with short sentences. This helps in understanding how finger spelling integrates into broader ASL communication.

Peer Review Sessions: Practice finger spelling with a peer or group. Take turns spelling and reading words or sentences. The feedback from peers can be invaluable in identifying areas for improvement.

Being able to accurately read finger spelling from others is as important as being able to spell yourself. This skill requires practice and attention to detail. The following tips and exercises are designed to enhance your ability to read finger spelling effectively.

Focus on the Handshape, Not the Finger Movement: When watching someone finger spell, concentrate on the overall handshape rather than trying to track each finger movement. This helps in recognizing the letter more quickly.

Watch the Whole Word: Instead of focusing on individual letters, try to see the word as a whole. With practice, you'll start to recognize patterns and shapes of common words.

Contextual Reading: Practice reading finger spelling within the context of a sentence or conversation. This helps in understanding how finger spelling fits into overall communication.

Silent Reading: Avoid the temptation to mouth the letters as you read them. This encourages reliance on visual cues alone, which is essential for fluent ASL communication.

Reading Practice from Various Sources: Try reading finger spelling from different people and sources. Everyone has a slightly different style of finger spelling, and exposure to this variety can improve your reading skills.

Transcription Exercise: Watch a finger spelling video and write down what is being spelled. Check your accuracy afterwards. This exercise helps in reinforcing your reading skills.

Flashcard Practice: Use flashcards with finger spelled words. Try to read the word quickly and then check your answer. This can be a good practice for quick recognition.

Week II: Essential Skills

Lesson 6: Pronouns in ASL

1. Personal Pronouns

'I/Me': To indicate 'I' or 'me', point your index finger towards your chest. This is a simple yet clear sign used universally in ASL.

'You': Point your index finger directly at the person you are addressing to indicate 'you'. Make sure to establish eye contact to ensure clarity of communication.

'He/She': To refer to another person (he or she), point your index finger towards the space where that person is or was. If the person is not present, establish a spatial reference point and point there whenever you refer to that person.

'We': To sign 'we', sweep your index finger or a flat handshape from your chest outward, towards the direction of the group included in 'we'. The movement may vary depending on the size of the group.

31

'They': Indicate 'they' by pointing with your index finger to an area off to the side, typically where the group you're referring to is or would be. You can also use a sweeping motion with your index finger or a flat handshape to encompass a larger group.

'It': For the pronoun 'it', point your index finger towards the object or direction of the item or concept being referred to. The context of the conversation usually makes it clear what 'it' refers to.

2. Possessive Pronouns

MY/MINE YOUR/YOURS MYSELF HIS THEIR/THRIRS HERS/ITS

'My/Mine': To sign 'my' or 'mine', use an open flat handshape and touch the palm or fingers to your chest. This sign is a possessive indicator that is straightforward and widely used.

'Your/Yours': Point an open flat hand toward the person you are addressing. The palm orientation and the direction of the movement indicate possession.

'His/Hers': To indicate 'his' or 'hers', point with an open hand towards the space representing that person. If the person is present, direct the open hand towards them. The context of the conversation will typically make clear whose possession is being referred to.

'Our/Ours': For 'our' or 'ours', use an open handshape, and move it in a small circular motion in front of the chest area. This sign represents shared possession among the group included in the 'our'.

'Their/Theirs': Indicate 'their' or 'theirs' by pointing with an open hand towards the space where the group you're referring to is or would be. If the group is not physically present, establish a spatial reference point and point there.

3. Reflexive Pronouns

'Myself': To sign 'myself', point your thumb towards your chest with an A-handshape (closed fist with the thumb extended), then move the hand in a small circular motion. This motion signifies that the action is directed towards oneself.

'Yourself': For 'yourself', point the A-handshape towards the person you are addressing and make the same circular motion. The direction of the movement towards the other person indicates the reflexive nature of the action.

'Himself/Herself': To indicate 'himself' or 'herself', point the A-handshape towards the space representing that person (if they are not present) and execute the circular motion. The space used should be consistent with where you have established that person spatially in your conversation.

'Ourselves': To express 'ourselves', use the A-handshape and move it in a circular motion in front of the body, encompassing the area that represents the group included in 'ourselves'. This motion indicates that the action pertains to the entire group.

'Themselves': Sign 'themselves' by pointing the A-handshape towards the space where the group you're referring to is or would be, and perform the circular motion. This conveys that the action is related back to the group.

Incorporating Facial Expressions: Facial expressions can enhance the meaning of reflexive pronouns. A neutral or self-reflective expression often complements these signs.

4. Demonstrative Pronouns

THAT   THESE/THOSE   THIS

'This': To indicate 'this', extend your index finger and point to a nearby object or person. The proximity of the item or individual is key here; 'this' is used for things that are physically close or within easy reach.

'That': For 'that', the same pointing gesture is used, but the arm is extended further, indicating something that is farther away. The direction and reach of your pointing convey the distance and location of the object or person.

'These': To convey 'these', use a flat hand or slightly curved handshape and make a small sweeping motion to encompass several nearby items or people. This plural form indicates multiple objects or individuals that are close to the signer.

'Those': Sign 'those' by using a similar sweeping motion as 'these', but with the arm extended to indicate items or people that are at a distance. This gesture can encompass a larger area or range, signifying that the objects or individuals are not in the immediate vicinity.

Eye Gaze and Body Orientation: When using demonstrative pronouns, your eye gaze and body orientation help to reinforce the location and identity of what you are referring to. Make sure to look at and orient your body toward the object or person while signing.

Contextual Usage: Demonstrative pronouns are often context-dependent. Their meaning can change based on the surrounding signs and the physical context of the conversation. Practice using these pronouns in various scenarios to understand how their meanings can shift.

Practice Exercises: Engage in exercises where you describe scenes using demonstrative pronouns. Place objects around you at different distances and practice referring to them using 'this', 'that', 'these', and 'those'.

Combining with Descriptive Signs: Often, demonstrative pronouns are used in conjunction with descriptive signs. Practice combining these pronouns with adjectives and verbs to create more complex sentences.

Spatial Consistency: When using demonstrative pronouns in a conversation, maintain spatial consistency. If you refer to something as 'that' (far away), continue to use the same spatial reference for the same object throughout the conversation.

Real-life Application: Apply these pronouns in real-life situations. For instance, when shopping, at work, or in social settings, use demonstrative pronouns to refer to items or people around you.

5. Interrogative Pronouns

HOW

WHAT

'**How**': To sign 'how', place both open hands in front of you, palms up, and then rotate them inwards in small circular motions. The facial expression is typically inquisitive, with raised eyebrows.

'**Who**': To sign 'who', place your hand at your forehead with your thumb and index finger extended and the rest of your fingers curled in, and then wiggle your fingers. A questioning facial expression, usually with eyebrows lowered, accompanies this sign.

'**What**': For 'what', hold both hands out, palms up, and shrug your shoulders slightly. This sign often goes with raised eyebrows and a tilted head to indicate a question.

WHEN

WHERE

'Where': To ask 'where', use the index finger to point at different locations, typically accompanied by a sweeping movement. The eyebrows are usually raised, and the head may be tilted, emphasizing the questioning nature.

'When': Sign 'when' by pointing your index finger upwards and spiraling it in a small circular motion. A curious or questioning expression, often with raised eyebrows, characterizes this sign.

'Why': The sign for 'why' involves forming a 'Y' handshape (with the thumb and pinky extended, and the other fingers curled in) and then rotating it back and forth at the wrist. Accompany this sign with a questioning facial expression, usually with eyebrows furrowed.

6. Incorporating Pronouns in Sentences

Using Personal Pronouns in Statements: For example, to say "I am a teacher," you would sign 'I/ME TEACHER' while pointing to yourself during the 'I/ME' sign. Similarly, "You are a student" would be signed as 'YOU STUDENT' with the point directed towards the person you are addressing.

Incorporating Possessive Pronouns: In a sentence like "This is my book," you would sign 'THIS MY BOOK', using the open handshape touching your chest for 'my'. For "Her car is new," sign 'HER CAR NEW', pointing to the space representing 'her'.

Using Reflexive Pronouns: An example sentence could be, "He introduced himself," which in ASL would be signed as 'HE INTRODUCE HIMSELF', with the reflexive pronoun sign directing back towards the space representing 'he'.

Employing Demonstrative Pronouns: In a sentence like "I want that apple," you would sign 'I WANT THAT APPLE', with 'THAT' being directed towards the apple's location.

Forming Questions with Interrogative Pronouns: For a question like "Where is your brother?" you would sign 'YOUR BROTHER WHERE', with raised eyebrows during the 'WHERE' sign.

7. Practice Exercises

Sentence Reconstruction: Take sentences written in English that heavily use pronouns and reconstruct them in ASL. Focus on the correct translation and placement of pronouns in the sentence structure.

Pronoun Identification: Watch videos of ASL conversations and identify the pronouns used. Write down the sentences you see and highlight the pronouns, noting their types (personal, possessive, reflexive, etc.).

Role-Playing Dialogues: Engage in role-playing activities where you deliberately use a variety of pronouns. For instance, create scenarios such as a family dinner, a classroom setting, or a meeting, and use appropriate pronouns in your conversation.

Matching Pronouns to Pictures: Use a set of pictures or scenarios and practice assigning the correct pronouns to each. For example, show a picture of a person with a dog and sign 'His dog is cute' or 'HER DOG CUTE'.

Fill-in-the-Blank: Create or find ASL worksheets where you fill in the blank with the appropriate pronoun. This can be a mix of written English and ASL gloss (the written form of ASL signs).

Comprehension Activities: Listen to or watch a story in ASL and then answer questions about it using pronouns. For example, "Who went to the store?" or "Whose book was lost?"

Translation Practice: Translate short paragraphs from English to ASL, focusing on the accurate and appropriate use of pronouns. Pay attention to the ASL sentence structure, which often differs from English.

Pronoun Substitution Game: With a group, practice substituting pronouns in sentences. One person signs a sentence using a noun, and the next person substitutes the noun with the correct pronoun.

Memory Game with Pronouns: Use flashcards with various pronouns and related signs. Flip them over and find matching pairs, signing the pronoun each time you turn over a card.

Creating Personal Stories: Create and sign a personal story or narrative, using a variety of pronouns. This helps in practicing pronoun use in a natural, flowing context.

8. Common Mistakes and How to Avoid Them

Confusing Possessive and Personal Pronouns: One common error is mixing up possessive and personal pronouns, like signing 'my' instead of 'I'. To avoid this, focus on the specific handshapes and movements for each type of pronoun and practice them separately until they are firmly differentiated in your mind.

Incorrect Body Orientation: Another mistake is incorrect body orientation when using pronouns, which can change the meaning of the sentence. Always remember to orient your body towards the person or object you are referring to. Practicing in front of a mirror or recording yourself can help correct this.

Misusing Reflexive Pronouns: Reflexive pronouns require the action to reflect back to the subject. Ensure you use the correct hand movement to indicate this, and avoid directing the action away from the subject.

Over-Reliance on English Grammar: Trying to directly translate English grammar into ASL can lead to errors, as ASL has its own grammatical structure. Be mindful of ASL syntax, especially in the placement and use of pronouns.

Neglecting Facial Expressions and Eye Gaze: Not using appropriate facial expressions and eye gaze, especially with interrogative pronouns, can make your questions unclear. Practice using your facial expressions and eye gaze to reinforce the meaning of your signs.

Avoiding Practice with Real Conversations: Relying solely on theoretical or structured practice can be less effective. Engage in real conversations where you can naturally use and adapt pronouns in various contexts.

Lesson 7: Number Basic

Numbers 1 through 20

Number 1: Extend the index finger, keeping the rest of the fingers closed and the thumb alongside the palm. The palm faces outward.

Number 2: Extend the index and middle fingers, keeping them together with the other fingers closed and the thumb tucked in. The palm faces outward.

Number 3: Extend the thumb, index, and middle fingers, while keeping the ring and pinky fingers closed. The palm faces outward.

Number 4: Extend all fingers while keeping the thumb tucked in. The palm faces outward, displaying all four fingers.

Number 5: Open your hand fully with all fingers spread out and the thumb extended. The palm faces outward, resembling a 'stop' sign.

Number 6: Form a circle with the thumb and the pinky finger, extending them while keeping the other fingers closed. The palm faces outward.

Number 7: Extend the thumb, index, and middle fingers, then hook the index finger slightly. The palm faces outward, with the ring and pinky fingers closed.

Number 8: Extend the thumb and index finger, keeping them slightly apart, and fold the other fingers into the palm. The palm faces outward.

Number 9: Curl the index finger towards the palm and extend the thumb, keeping the other fingers closed. The palm faces outward.

Number 10: Extend the thumb and wave it back and forth. This sign is like a combination of '1' and '0'.

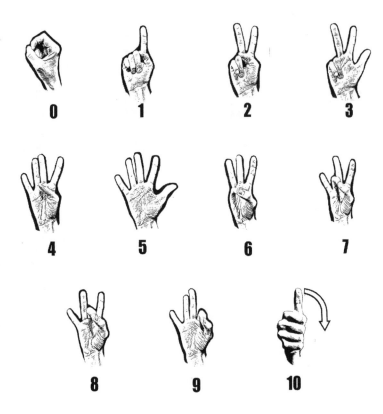

Common Mistakes:

Unclear Handshapes: Practice forming each number with a clear and distinct handshape to avoid confusion, especially between numbers that have similar formations like 6 and 9.

Numbers 11 through 20

Number 11: Flick the index finger upward twice. The hand starts with a similar position to the number 1, but the movement is key.

Number 12: Flick the index and middle fingers upward together twice. This sign starts similarly to the number 2.

Number 13: Bring the thumb to the side of the index finger, then flick the index finger upward while keeping the rest of the fingers closed.

Number 14: Similar to 13, but with the thumb touching the side of the middle finger. Flick the middle finger upward.

Number 15: The thumb is placed on the side of the pinky finger, and the pinky is flicked upward.

Number 16: Form a '6' handshape (thumb and pinky extended, forming a circle) and twist the wrist inward twice.

Number 17: Start with the '7' handshape (thumb, index, and middle fingers extended) and twist the wrist inward twice.

Number 18: Begin with the '8' handshape (thumb and index finger extended, slightly apart) and twist the wrist inward twice.

Number 19: Start with the '9' handshape (index finger curled, thumb extended) and twist the wrist inward twice.

Number 20: Touch the tips of your thumb and index finger together while keeping the other fingers extended, resembling the 'OK' sign or the letter 'G' in ASL.

Common Mistakes:

Wrist Twisting: For numbers 16-19, pay attention to the wrist-twisting motion, as it is a distinguishing feature for these numbers.

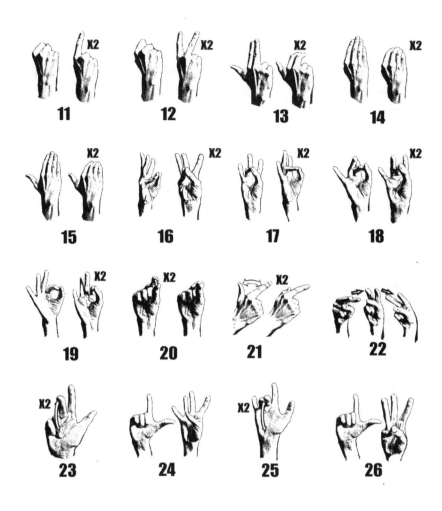

Counting in Tens and Hundreds

Tens (20-90): For numbers in the tens, start with the sign for the first digit and then move into the position for a zero. For example, for '20', sign '2' and then transition to '0'. For '30', sign '3' followed by '0', and so on. This pattern continues up to '90'.

Hundreds (100-900): To sign hundreds, first sign the number of hundreds (1-9) and then sign the 'C' handshape, which represents 'hundred'. For example, '100' is signed with the '1' handshape followed by the 'C' handshape. The pattern is similar for '200', '300', and up to '900'.

Thousands (1,000-9,000): For thousands, begin with the number (1-9) and then sign the 'M' handshape, which stands for 'thousand'. For example, '1,000' is signed by first showing the '1' handshape and then transitioning to the 'M' handshape. This pattern is consistent for '2,000', '3,000', and so forth up to '9,000'.

Larger Numbers: For numbers larger than 9,000, sign the full number in sequence. For example, '10,000' is signed as '1-0-0-0-0', and '21,300' is signed as '2-1-3-0-0'.

Use of Space: When signing larger numbers, use space effectively to indicate the scale of the number. This can involve broader movements for thousands and more confined movements for hundreds.

Clear Handshapes: Ensure that each handshape for the digits is clear and distinct, especially when signing complex numbers that involve multiple digits.

Common Mistakes:

Confusing Handshapes: Pay attention to not confuse the handshapes for 'hundred' (C) and 'thousand' (M).

Inconsistent Movements: Ensure consistent and clear movements, especially when transitioning between digits in larger numbers.

Age: To indicate age, combine the sign for the number with the sign for 'year old'. For instance, to sign '25 years old', you would sign '25' followed by the ASL sign for 'year old', which involves brushing the fingers of the dominant hand downward along the chin.

Year: For 'year', the sign is made by forming an 'S' handshape with both hands and then moving them in a circular motion in front of the body, as if to show the passing of a year. To sign a specific year, like '1995', you would sign each individual number followed by the 'year' sign.

Time: Indicating time involves pointing to the wrist (as if indicating a watch for 'o'clock') and then signing the specific hour and minute. For example, '3 o'clock' is signed by first pointing to the wrist and then signing '3'.

Date: To sign 'date', you combine the sign for 'day', which is an 'D' handshape tapped against the palm, with the numerical date. For instance, 'July 4th' would be signed as 'JULY' followed by '4' and then the sign for 'day'.

Money: Money amounts combine the number with the sign for 'dollars' or 'cents'. 'Dollars' is signed by rubbing the thumb against the index finger, while 'cents' involves a 'C' handshape moving in a circular motion. For example, '$20' is signed as '20' followed by the sign for 'dollars'.

Ordinal Numbers: Ordinal numbers (first, second, third, etc.) involve adding a twisting motion to the number. For example, 'first' is signed by forming the number '1' and then twisting the wrist.

Common Mistakes:

Confusing 'Day' and 'Date': Be clear on the difference between signing 'day' and a specific 'date'.

Incorrectly Signing 'Time' and 'Hour': Distinguish between signing 'time' in general and specific 'hours'.

Misrepresenting 'Year': Ensure the circular motion for 'year' is clear and distinct when combined with specific years.

Incorporating Numbers into Sentences

Placement of Numbers in Sentences: In ASL, numbers usually come after the subject and before the verb. For example, "She has three dogs" would be signed as 'SHE THREE DOGS HAVE'. This structure helps to maintain clarity and flow in ASL syntax.

Using Numbers in Time Expressions: When expressing time, the number typically comes before the time indicator. For example, "It's 2 o'clock" would be signed as '2 TIME' (with 'TIME' being indicated by pointing to the wrist).

Numbers in Dates: For dates, sign the number after stating the month. For instance, "July 4th" would be signed as 'JULY 4'. If including the year, the year would follow the date, such as 'JULY 4 2021'.

Describing Age: When describing age, sign the number followed by the sign for 'year old'. For example, "I am 25 years old" would be signed as 'I 25 YEAR OLD'.

Discussing Money: In sentences involving money, the number should precede the sign for 'dollars' or 'cents'. For example, "That costs $15" would be signed as 'THAT 15 DOLLARS COST'.

COST   **MONEY**

PAY

DOLLAR   **BUY**

Ordinal Numbers in Sentences: Use ordinal numbers to indicate order. For example, "He finished second" would be signed as 'HE SECOND FINISH', with a twisting motion on 'SECOND'.

Common Mistakes:

Direct Translation from English: Avoid the temptation to directly translate English sentence structure into ASL, as this can lead to grammatical errors.

Misplacement of Numbers: Ensure numbers are placed correctly in relation to other elements in the sentence.

Forgetting Number Agreement: In ASL, the form of the number must agree with what it is describing. For instance, when discussing '3 cats', ensure the sign for '3' aligns with the sign for 'cats'.

Practice Exercises

Counting Drills: Practice counting from 1 to 100 in ASL. Start by counting slowly, then gradually increase your speed as you become more comfortable.

Backward Counting: Count backward from 20 to 1. This helps in familiarizing yourself with the handshapes and transitions between numbers in reverse order.

Flashcard Matching: Use flashcards with numbers on one side and their corresponding ASL signs on the other. This exercise aids in visual recognition and memory.

Number Translation: Translate written numbers into ASL signs. Start with simple numbers and gradually move on to more complex ones, like dates and large quantities.

Signing Dates and Times: Practice signing different dates and times, both current and historical. For instance, sign your birthday, today's date, or a significant historical date.

Money Amounts: Work on signing different amounts of money. You could use real-life scenarios, like pricing items or discussing a budget.

Ordinal Number Practice: Incorporate ordinal numbers into sentences. For instance, discuss finishing orders in a race or rankings in a list.

Age Descriptions: Describe the ages of family members or famous people using ASL. This helps practice the combination of number signs with the 'year old' sign.

Role-playing Shopping Scenarios: Create scenarios where you discuss prices, quantities, and totals, such as in a shopping or restaurant setting.

Timed Number Recall: Have someone say a number, and then quickly sign it in ASL. This exercise helps with rapid recognition and signing of numbers.

Creating Number Stories: Develop short stories or narratives that include a variety of numbers. This can be a fun way to practice numbers in a more dynamic context.

Peer Review Sessions: Practice signing numbers with a partner and provide each other with feedback. This can be helpful in identifying and correcting mistakes.

Tips for Fluid Number Signing

Gradual Increase in Speed: Start practicing at a slower pace to ensure accuracy in handshapes and movements. Gradually increase your speed as you become more comfortable, but never at the expense of clarity.

Smooth Transitions: Focus on making smooth transitions between numbers, especially when counting in sequence or signing complex numbers. Practice transitioning without abrupt stops or awkward pauses.

Consistent Palm Orientation: Pay attention to the orientation of your palm, as it can change the meaning of the number. Practice maintaining a consistent orientation that is clear to the viewer.

Use of Space: Be aware of the space in front of you when signing numbers. Larger movements can be used for emphasis or to indicate larger quantities, but they should still be controlled and deliberate.

Repetition and Muscle Memory: Repeat number signs regularly to build muscle memory. This will help your hands to naturally form the correct shapes and movements.

Mirror Practice: Practice in front of a mirror to get visual feedback on your signing. This can help you adjust your handshapes, movements, and facial expressions.

Record and Review: Record yourself signing numbers and watch the playback. This allows you to critique your own performance and make necessary improvements.

Relax Your Hands: Avoid tensing your hands and fingers. Keeping your hands relaxed will help your movements to be more fluid and natural.

Facial Expressions and Body Language: Incorporate appropriate facial expressions and body language. This adds to the overall clarity and can provide additional context, especially in conversational settings.

Seek Feedback: If possible, get feedback from experienced ASL users. They can provide valuable insights into your signing style and offer suggestions for improvement.

Contextual Practice: Use numbers in real-life contexts as much as possible. Whether it's discussing prices, dates, or quantities, real-world practice is invaluable for achieving fluency.

Finger Dexterity Exercises: Engage in exercises to improve finger dexterity. This can include activities outside of ASL practice, like playing a musical instrument or typing, which can improve your overall hand and finger agility.

Common Mistakes and How to Avoid Them

When learning to sign numbers in ASL, certain common errors can occur. Being aware of these mistakes and knowing how to avoid them can significantly enhance your signing accuracy.

Confusing Similar-Looking Numbers: Numbers like '6' and '9', or '15' and '50' can look similar. To avoid confusion, practice these numbers side by side and pay close attention to hand orientation and movement. Clear, distinct movements are crucial for differentiating these numbers.

Incorrect Hand Orientation: The direction in which your palm faces can change the meaning of a number. Make sure to learn and consistently use the correct palm orientation for each number. Practicing in front of a mirror can help you self-monitor and correct your orientation.

Inconsistent Handshapes: Forgetting to fully extend or properly position fingers can lead to miscommunication. Regular practice and muscle memory exercises can help maintain consistent handshapes.

Rushing Through Numbers: Speeding through numbers before mastering them can result in unclear signs. Slow down your practice and focus on clarity before gradually increasing your speed.

Incorrect Use of Space: Not using space effectively, especially for larger numbers, can make your signs difficult to understand. Practice using the space in front of you deliberately, ensuring your movements are visible and clear.

Neglecting Non-Manual Cues: Remember that facial expressions and body language play a part in number signing, especially in conversational contexts. Be expressive and use your body to support the clarity of your signs.

Over-Complication of Large Numbers: When signing large numbers, some learners over-complicate the process. Break down large numbers into smaller segments and practice signing them in sequence to maintain clarity.

Not Seeking Feedback: Practicing in isolation without feedback can reinforce incorrect habits. Whenever possible, practice with others, especially those who are fluent in ASL, and seek their feedback.

Lack of Contextual Practice: Practicing numbers in isolation can lead to difficulties when using them in sentences or conversations. Incorporate number signs into full sentences and real-life scenarios to improve your practical skills.

Forgetting Sequential Flow: In ASL, numbers often follow a sequential flow, especially in counting or listing. Ensure that your transition between numbers is logical and smooth.

Lesson 8: Days of the Week. Tenses and Time

Signing Days of the Week

Monday: The sign for Monday is made by forming an 'M' handshape (three fingers extended, thumb over the pinky) and rotating your wrist in a small circular motion. This sign is reminiscent of the first letter of "Monday."

Tuesday: For Tuesday, use a 'T' handshape (index finger up, thumb across the palm) and make the same circular wrist motion. This movement is akin to the initial letter of "Tuesday."

Wednesday: Wednesday's sign uses a 'W' handshape (fingers forming a 'W', thumb underneath) with the same circular wrist motion, representing the first letter of "Wednesday."

Thursday: For Thursday, the handshape is a 'T' (similar to Tuesday), but you add an 'H' movement by wiggling the two fingers upward, signifying the 'H' in "Thursday."

Friday: The sign for Friday involves an 'F' handshape (index finger and thumb touching, other fingers extended) with the familiar circular wrist motion, indicating the first letter of "Friday."

Saturday: Saturday starts with an 'S' handshape (a fist, thumb in front of fingers) and the wrist makes the usual circular motion. This handshape corresponds to the initial letter of "Saturday."

Sunday: To indicate Sunday, use an open palm handshape, facing forward, and circle the wrist. This sign is symbolic of the sun and the first letter of "Sunday."

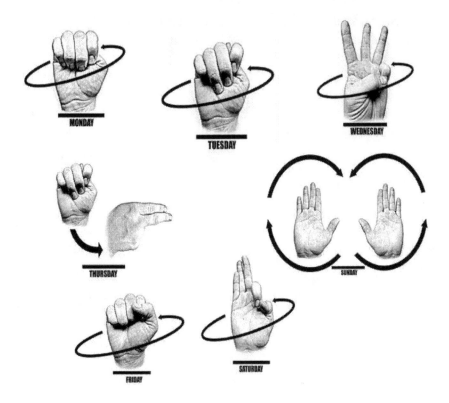

Tenses in ASL

Present Tense: The present tense in ASL is usually indicated by the context of the conversation. There is no specific sign for the present tense; it is understood through the immediacy of the situation or the signing.

Past Tense: To indicate the past tense, signs like 'BEFORE', 'PAST', or 'YESTERDAY' are often used at the beginning or end of a sentence. For example, "I ate" would be signed as 'YESTERDAY I EAT'. Facial expressions and body language leaning backward can also indicate past tense.

Future Tense: The future tense is typically indicated by signs such as 'WILL', 'FUTURE', or 'TOMORROW'. These signs are used at the beginning or end of a sentence. For example, "I will go" can be signed as 'FUTURE I GO'. Leaning forward slightly while signing can also denote future actions.

Time Signs to Indicate Tense: Specific time signs like 'NEXT-WEEK', 'LAST-YEAR', or 'SOON' can also establish tense. For instance, 'NEXT-WEEK I GO VACATION' clearly indicates a future event.

Non-Manual Markers: Facial expressions, head tilting, and eye gaze play a significant role in conveying tense. Raised eyebrows and a forward head tilt often accompany future tense, while a relaxed or neutral expression with a slight backward tilt can indicate past tense.

Common Mistakes:

Omitting Time Indicators: Not using time signs like 'YESTERDAY' or 'TOMORROW' can lead to ambiguous sentences.

Misusing Non-Manual Markers: Incorrect facial expressions or body language can convey the wrong tense. Pay close attention to these aspects during practice.

Expressing Time of Day

Morning: The sign for 'morning' is made by holding your non-dominant arm horizontally in front of you, representing the horizon, and then taking your dominant hand in a flat shape from below the horizon to above it, like the sun rising.

Afternoon: To indicate 'afternoon', use the same 'horizon' arm as a base and move your dominant hand in a flat shape over the horizon, indicating the sun moving through the sky.

Evening: 'Evening' is signed by holding your non-dominant arm horizontally and moving your dominant hand in a flat shape from above the horizon to just below it, representing the sun setting.

Night: For 'night', simply hold your dominant hand with fingers and thumb extended and slightly spread, palm down, and then flip it over to palm up, suggesting the change from day to night.

Telling Specific Times: To tell specific times, first sign the hour part and then the minute part. For instance, 3:30 would be signed '3 HOUR 30 MINUTE'. The sign for 'hour' is tapping your dominant wrist with your non-dominant index finger, as if indicating a watch.

A.M. and P.M.: To specify A.M. or P.M., you can sign 'MORNING' or 'NIGHT' respectively after stating the time. Alternatively, the context of the conversation usually makes the time of day clear.

Discussing Days and Dates

Combining Days with Dates: When discussing a specific date, you typically sign the day of the week followed by the date. For instance, "Friday, July 9th" would be signed as 'FRIDAY JULY 9'. The day of the week is signed first, followed by the month, and then the date.

Using Ordinal Numbers for Dates: Dates often require ordinal numbers (like '1st', '2nd', '3rd', etc.). In ASL, you sign the number followed by a twisting motion to indicate its ordinal form. For instance, 'JULY 4' for "July 4th", with a twisting motion on '4'.

Signing Years: When including the year, sign it after the date. For example, "May 15th, 2021" would be signed as 'MAY 15 YEAR 2021', with the year signed in a digit-by-digit format.

Discussing Ranges of Dates: To discuss a range, such as "from June 1st to June 10th", sign 'JUNE 1 START, JUNE 10 FINISH'. Use signs like 'START' and 'FINISH' to indicate the beginning and end of the range.

Time-Related Phrases

Yesterday: The sign for 'yesterday' involves holding your dominant hand in a fist with your thumb extended over your shoulder, suggesting something in the past.

Today: To indicate 'today', form a 'Y' handshape with your dominant hand and move it down in a small arc in front of your body. This sign can also be interpreted as 'now' or 'currently'.

Tomorrow: 'Tomorrow' is signed by pointing your index finger forward from the side of your forehead, suggesting something coming up or in the future.

Last Week: For 'last week', use a 'W' handshape and move it backward over your shoulder in a small arc. This gesture indicates moving back in time to the previous week.

Next Week: 'Next week' is signed by using the 'W' handshape and moving it forward from your body, indicating moving forward in time.

Last Month: Use an 'M' handshape and move it backward over your shoulder for 'last month', indicating a time in the past month.

Next Month: 'Next month' is signed by using an 'M' handshape and moving it forward from your body, suggesting the upcoming month.

Soon: To indicate 'soon', hold your index finger up near your head and waggle it back and forth slightly. This sign conveys a sense of something happening in the near future.

Later: The sign for 'later' involves taking your 'L' handshape and moving it from your thumb side outward, suggesting something happening after a while.

Now/Immediately: To convey 'now' or 'immediately', tap your hands together with flat handshapes, indicating the present or immediate time.

Lesson 9: Most Common Signs

In addition to specific topics like days of the week and time expressions, it's important for learners of American Sign Language (ASL) to become familiar with a core set of signs that are most commonly used in everyday communication. This section will introduce and describe some of these essential signs.

Greetings and Farewells: Basic signs such as 'HELLO', 'GOODBYE', 'GOOD MORNING', 'GOOD NIGHT', and 'THANK YOU' are fundamental in any conversation. Practice these signs to greet people appropriately and show politeness.

Basic Questions: Signs for 'WHO', 'WHAT', 'WHERE', 'WHEN', 'WHY', and 'HOW' are crucial for asking questions. Mastering these signs is key to engaging in meaningful conversations.

Everyday Verbs: Common verbs like 'GO', 'COME', 'EAT', 'DRINK', 'SLEEP', 'SEE', 'HEAR', 'LIKE', and 'WANT' are used frequently. Familiarize yourself with these to express daily activities and desires.

GO

HEARING **WANT**

Relationships: Signs for 'BOY', 'GIRL', 'MAN', 'WOMAN' are often used in personal conversations.

MAN

Emotions and Adjectives: Learn signs for common emotions like 'HAPPY', 'SAD', 'ANGRY', 'TIRED', and adjectives like 'BIG', 'SMALL', 'HOT', 'COLD', 'NEW', 'OLD'. These help in describing feelings and characteristics.

Practical Items and Locations: Signs for everyday items and places like 'HOUSE', 'CAR', 'WORK', 'SCHOOL', 'STORE', 'FOOD', 'WATER', 'PHONE' are also essential.

Time Concepts: Basic time concepts including 'DAY', 'NIGHT', 'WEEK', 'MONTH', 'YEAR', 'NOW', 'LATER', 'SOON', 'BEFORE', and 'AFTER' are important for discussing schedules and planning.

Directions and Prepositions: Common signs for directions and prepositions like 'UP', 'DOWN', 'LEFT', 'RIGHT', 'IN', 'OUT', 'UNDER', 'OVER', 'BESIDE', 'BETWEEN' are useful in giving and understanding directions.

NOW

LEFT

RIGHT

Lesson 10: Sentence structure. Questions & Answers

While ASL often employs a Subject-Verb-Object (SVO) structure, flexibility in sentence construction allows for emphasis and clarity based on context. This section expands on how sentence structure in ASL can vary and adapt to different communication needs.

Object-Subject-Verb (OSV) Structure: Sometimes, especially for emphasis or clarity, ASL uses an OSV structure. For instance, "The apple, the boy is eating" could be signed as 'APPLE, BOY EAT', emphasizing the apple first.

Subject-Object-Verb (SOV) Structure: In certain contexts, especially in storytelling or descriptive narratives, ASL may use an SOV structure. For example, "The boy the apple eats" to emphasize the action on the object.

Time-Topic-Comment Structure: Time indicators often come at the beginning of sentences in ASL. For example, "Tomorrow, I will go to the store" would be signed 'TOMORROW, I GO STORE'.

Topicalization for Emphasis: When a particular part of the sentence needs emphasis, it is brought to the beginning, followed by the rest of the sentence. For example, to emphasize the location, "I study at the library" can be signed 'LIBRARY, I STUDY'.

Conditional Clauses: In conditional sentences, the condition is typically stated first, followed by the outcome. For example, "If it rains, we will stay home" would be signed 'RAIN IF, HOME STAY WE'.

Negation at the End: Sometimes, negation comes at the end of the sentence for emphasis. For example, "I don't like apples" could be signed 'I LIKE APPLES NOT', with a head shake on 'NOT'.

Practice Exercises:

Reordering Sentences: Practice rearranging sentences in different structures (SVO, OSV, SOV) to see how it changes the emphasis.

Emphasizing Elements: Create sentences that emphasize different elements (like subject, object, or verb) and practice signing them.

Conditional Sentences: Form conditional sentences in ASL, ensuring the correct structure is followed.

Common Mistakes:

Rigid Adherence to SVO: Avoid sticking rigidly to the SVO structure; ASL is more flexible.

Overlooking Non-Manual Markers: Remember that facial expressions and body language often support the sentence structure and should align with the intended meaning.

Usage of Topicalization: In ASL, topicalization is used to set the scene or bring attention to the main subject of the sentence. For example, in a sentence like "My sister, she is very smart," you would sign 'MY SISTER, SHE SMART VERY'.

Non-Manual Markers in Topicalization: Raised eyebrows and a slight forward lean are often used when introducing the topic. This helps to indicate to the viewer that a topic is being set before the comment is made.

Pause Between Topic and Comment: A brief pause is usually made after introducing the topic and before signing the comment. This pause helps to differentiate the topic from the rest of the sentence.

WH-Questions

WH-questions in American Sign Language (ASL) are crucial for seeking specific information. These questions involve the use of WH-signs such as 'who', 'what', 'where', 'when', 'why', and 'how', and are accompanied by distinctive non-manual signals.

Lowered Eyebrows and Forward Lean: Unlike yes/no questions, WH-questions are characterized by lowered eyebrows throughout the question. A slight forward lean of the head is also common, indicating the inquisitive nature of the question.

Placement of WH-Signs: The WH-signs can be placed either at the beginning or the end of the sentence. For example, "What is your name?" could be signed as 'WHAT YOUR NAME?' or 'YOUR NAME WHAT?', with both versions involving a furrowing of the eyebrows.

Holding the WH-Sign: When posing a WH-question, it's common to hold the WH-sign (like 'WHO', 'WHERE', etc.) a bit longer to emphasize the question and signal that a response is expected.

Using 'NOT' and 'NONE': The signs 'NOT' and 'NONE' are commonly used to negate a sentence in ASL. 'NOT' is usually signed by bringing the index and middle fingers of the dominant hand sharply down onto the thumb of the same hand. 'NONE' is signed by forming an 'O' shape with the thumb and fingers and then opening it into a flat hand facing downward.

Head Shake for Emphasis: Along with the signs for negation, a side-to-side head shake is often used as a non-manual marker to emphasize the negation. This head shake usually occurs while signing 'NOT' or 'NONE'. The placement of 'NOT' can vary. It often comes at the end of the sentence, but it can also be placed immediately before the verb or the concept being negated. For example, "I do not like apples" could be signed 'I NOT LIKE APPLES' or 'I LIKE APPLES

NOT', with a head shake during 'NOT'.

NOT

Using 'IF' and 'SUPPOSE': The signs 'IF' and 'SUPPOSE' are commonly used to start conditional sentences. 'IF' is signed by extending the index finger and bending it at the middle joint, while 'SUPPOSE' involves moving a 'C' handshape back and forth in front of the forehead.

Structure of Conditional Sentences: Typically, the condition is stated first using 'IF' or 'SUPPOSE', followed by the consequence or result. For example, "If it rains, we will cancel the trip" would be signed as 'IF RAIN, CANCEL TRIP WE'.

Non-Manual Markers: Conditional sentences in ASL often involve specific facial expressions, such as raised eyebrows when signing the condition, and a return to a neutral expression when signing the consequence.

Temporal Aspect Markers: For expressing future conditions and consequences, temporal aspect markers like 'WILL' or 'FUTURE' can be used to clarify the timing. For example, 'IF RAIN, FUTURE CANCEL TRIP WE'.

Week III: Day-to-day use

Lesson 11: Colors, Shapes, and Descriptors

Signing Colors

Red: Slide the index finger down your lips. This sign is reminiscent of applying lipstick, a common association with the color red.

Blue: Form a 'B' handshape (palm facing forward, fingers together, thumb across palm) and shake it at the wrist. Think of the blue sky, which is vast and expansive like the spread of the fingers.

Green: Make a 'G' handshape (index finger and thumb extended, other fingers folded) and shake it at the wrist. The 'G' can remind you of green grass.

Yellow: Form a 'Y' handshape (thumb and pinky extended, other fingers folded) and shake it at the wrist. The 'Y' can be associated with the bright rays of the sun, which is often yellow.

Black: Place your index finger against your forehead and pull it away. The sign is reminiscent of pulling down the brim of a black hat.

White: Place your hand on your chest and then pull it away, fingers spread. It's like showing a white shirt on your chest.

Orange: Squeeze your hand in front of your mouth as if squeezing an orange. This sign is a natural association with the fruit of the same color.

Purple: Make a 'P' handshape (middle finger bent over thumb, index finger extended) and shake it at the wrist. The circular shape of the 'P' can remind you of grapes, which are often purple.

Pink: Extend your middle finger and tap it on your chin. The sign can be remembered by associating it with pink lipstick.

Brown: Make a 'B' handshape and run it down the side of your face. This sign is similar to the motion of wiping dirt or mud, which is typically brown.

Gray: Wiggle your fingers in front of your face as you move your hand from side to side. The sign can be thought of as the unclear, hazy quality often associated with the color gray.

Shapes and Their Signs

Circle: Form an 'O' shape with your dominant hand and then trace a circular motion in the air. This action mimics the round shape of a circle.

Square: Use both hands to outline the four sides of a square in the air. Start with your index fingers and thumbs touching to form the top line, then move your hands down and apart to create the sides, and finally bring them together again to complete the bottom line.

Triangle: Use both index fingers to trace the outline of a triangle in the air. Start at the top point, move down to the bottom left corner, across to the bottom right corner, and then back up to the top.

Rectangle: Similar to the square, but make the side movements longer than the top and bottom movements, indicating the elongated shape of a rectangle.

Star: Wiggle your fingers on both hands while bringing them together in front of you to outline a star shape. This sign mimics the twinkling of a star.

Descriptive Adjectives

Big/Large: Show the concept of 'big' or 'large' by holding your hands apart, palms facing each other, and then moving them apart. The wider the movement, the larger the size you're indicating.

Small: Indicate 'small' by pinching your thumb and index finger together with the other fingers tucked in. The closer the pinch, the smaller the size.

Tall: To sign 'tall', hold your flat hand with fingers together, palm facing out, and move it vertically upward. The height of the hand indicates the height being described.

Short: 'Short' is signed by holding your hand horizontally, palm down, and then moving it downward slightly. The lower the hand, the shorter the height or length.

Thin/Slim: Use the edge of your hand (index finger side) to show something thin or slim, moving it vertically up and down.

Thick: To demonstrate 'thick', hold your hands parallel to each other with a gap in between, indicating the thickness.

Light (Weight): To sign something light in weight, mimic picking up something with ease using a gentle, upward hand movement.

Heavy: Indicate 'heavy' by pretending to lift something with effort, using a strained facial expression to emphasize the weight.

Describing Textures and Patterns

In American Sign Language (ASL), describing textures and patterns involves specific signs and expressions that convey the feel or appearance of an object. Here's how to sign some common textures and patterns:

Smooth: To indicate 'smooth', use your dominant hand to mimic a gentle, gliding motion over the other hand. This sign mimics the action of feeling a smooth surface.

Rough: Sign 'rough' by making a bumpy motion with your dominant hand over the palm of your non-dominant hand. The movement and facial expressions should suggest a coarse texture.

Striped: For 'striped', use an index finger to mimic drawing lines across your non-dominant hand or in the air. The motion imitates the pattern of stripes.

Spotted or Dotted: Show 'spotted' or 'dotted' by using the tip of your index finger to make dotting motions on your non-dominant hand or in the air, similar to depicting spots or dots.

Lesson 12: Family and Friends

Signing Family Members

Mother: Open your hand with fingers spread and thumb touching your chin, then move your hand away from your chin in a small arc. This sign is often associated with the traditional gesture of a mother cradling a baby.

Father: Similar to 'mother', but the open hand starts at the forehead instead of the chin. This sign is reminiscent of a paternal figure, often represented by the forehead in many cultures.

Sister: Combine the signs for 'girl' and 'same'. Start with the thumb of your open hand near your jawbone (the sign for 'girl'), then move to an 'L' handshape with your index and thumb fingers and link them together (the sign for 'same').

Brother: Similar to 'sister', start with the sign for 'boy' (a flat hand taps the forehead twice), followed by the 'same' sign, as described above.

Grandmother: Start with the sign for 'mother', then arc your hand out and forward in a gesture that suggests a line of descent.

Grandfather: As with 'grandmother', but start with the sign for 'father' and use the same outward arcing motion.

Aunt: Form the letter 'A' with your dominant hand (thumb alongside your index finger, other fingers curled), and circle it near your cheek.

Uncle: Form the letter 'U' (index and middle fingers extended, other fingers curled), and circle it near the side of your forehead.

Cousin: Form the letter 'C' and circle it near the side of your forehead. You can specify gender by starting at the chin for female cousins or the forehead for male cousins.

Child: Place your flat hands, palms facing each other, in front of you at waist height, then gently move them downward. This sign mimics the height and size of a child.

GRANDMA

GRANDPA

DAUGHTER

SON

SISTER

BROTHER

HUSBAND

WIFE

Describing Relationships

Marital Status:

Married: Form both hands into 'D' handshapes and join the ring fingers together. This sign symbolizes the wearing of wedding rings.

Single: Use an 'S' handshape (fist) and shake it side to side slightly. This sign represents being alone or single.

Divorced: Start with the sign for 'married', then sharply break the hands apart, symbolizing the end of the marriage.

In-Laws: Combine the sign for the specific family member with the sign for 'law'. For example, 'mother-in-law' would be the sign for 'mother' followed by 'law', which is signed by forming an 'L' with one hand and moving it in a small horizontal circle.

Stepfamily: Indicate a stepfamily relationship by signing the family member followed by 'step'. For example, 'stepmother' is signed as 'mother' followed by 'step', which is signed by tapping the heel of the palm with the other hand.

Adoption: The sign for 'adoption' involves mimicking the cradling of a baby (similar to the sign for 'baby') and then moving your hands outward, indicating taking in or receiving.

Boyfriend/Girlfriend: Sign 'boyfriend' or 'girlfriend' by using the signs for 'boy' or 'girl', followed by a bent 'B' handshape that moves back and forth from the chest, indicating a close romantic relationship.

Signing Types of Friends

Best Friend: Use the sign for 'FRIEND' (which is made by interlocking the index fingers of both hands) and then use your other fingers to show a number '1' on top of them, indicating 'number one' or 'best'.

Close Friend: Sign 'FRIEND' as usual, then pull your hands towards your chest after linking fingers, indicating a close, personal connection.

Classmate: Combine the sign for 'CLASS' (hands forming a 'C' shape, one on top of the other, moving in a circular motion) with 'MATE' (similar to the sign for 'FRIEND'). This signifies a peer in an educational setting.

Coworker: Start with the sign for 'WORK' (fists hitting each other in alternating movements), followed by 'MATE', to indicate a relationship formed through a shared workplace.

Neighbor: The sign for 'neighbor' involves forming the letter 'N' with both hands (index and middle fingers extended, touching at the tips) and then moving them from one side to the other. This motion represents proximity or living side by side.

Phrases and Expressions for Family and Friends

Family Gathering: To sign 'family gathering', first sign 'FAMILY' (with an 'F' handshape circled around to include a group) and then 'GATHER' (where both open hands come together in front of the body). This expression is used to describe a meeting or get-together of family members.

Friendship: The sign for 'friendship' is similar to 'FRIEND' but extended to emphasize a long-term or significant relationship. It's like linking the fingers of 'FRIEND' multiple times or using a more exaggerated movement.

Hang Out: To express 'hang out' in ASL, use the sign for 'SPEND-TIME' (where hands indicate passing time) with a relaxed facial expression, conveying casual social time spent with friends.

Get Together: Similar to 'family gathering', but more general. Sign 'GET' (by pulling hands towards the chest) and 'TOGETHER' (with both fists coming together).

Family Ties: For 'family ties', sign 'FAMILY' and then use a gesture that shows interconnectedness, like interlocking fingers or weaving hands together. This sign conveys the concept of strong familial bonds.

Lesson 13: Food and drink

Common Food Signs

Fruits

Apple: Mime twisting an apple from a tree with your hand.

Banana: Use your index finger to show the peeling of a banana.

Orange: Form a fist and squeeze it slightly, like squeezing an orange.

Vegetables

Carrot: Mime holding a carrot and breaking it in half.

Lettuce: Hold your hand flat and palm-up, then make a motion as if the leaves are sprouting up from your palm.

Tomato: Make a fist and touch your chin, then twist your hand, similar to the motion used for 'red'.

Meats

Chicken: Show the beak of a chicken with your thumb and index finger pecking.

Beef: Spell 'B' and then mime slicing meat.

Fish: Mime the movement of a fish swimming through water.

Dairy Products

Milk: Mime milking a cow with a squeezing motion.

Cheese: Hold both hands flat, palms facing each other, and then twist them as if you are lightly twisting a large block of cheese.

Egg: Form a 'C' handshape with one hand and a fist with the other, then tap the fist against the 'C' as if cracking an egg.

Grains

Bread: Mime slicing a loaf of bread.

Rice: Flick your index finger off your thumb repeatedly, indicating many small grains.

Pasta: Hold your hand flat and then make a twirling motion, as if twirling spaghetti on a fork.

Snacks

Chips: Use a flat hand to mimic picking up a chip and bringing it to your mouth.

Chocolate: Use the sign for 'C' near your mouth and then mimic breaking a bar.

Popcorn: Flick your fingers open from a fist, mimicking popcorn kernels popping.

Signing Beverages

Water: Form a 'W' handshape (three middle fingers up, thumb and pinkie tucked) and tap your chin. This sign mimics the act of drinking water.

Coffee: Mime the act of grinding coffee beans with one hand over the other. This sign reflects the traditional method of preparing coffee.

Tea: Mimic the act of dipping a tea bag with your index finger moving up and down. It's like steeping tea in a cup.

Milk: Similar to the sign for 'cow', mimic milking a cow by squeezing your hand open and closed. This sign originates from the source of milk.

Juice: Squeeze your hand in front of your mouth, similar to the sign for 'orange', but without the twisting motion. It's like squeezing juice from a fruit.

Soda: Pop the index finger off your thumb, mimicking the sound and action of opening a soda can.

Alcoholic Drinks: For general alcoholic drinks, mimic the action of tipping a glass to your mouth. For specific drinks like beer or wine, use the signs that represent these drinks specifically.

Preferences (Hot, Cold, Sweet, Bitter)

Hot: Wave your hand up from your mouth, as if feeling the steam rising from a hot beverage.

Cold: Shiver slightly while signing the drink to indicate coldness.

Sweet: Swipe your index finger across your lips, indicating sweetness.

Bitter: Make a face that shows distaste, and flick your index finger off your thumb from the corner of your mouth.

Meal-Related Signs

Breakfast: The sign for 'breakfast' involves miming the act of eating from a spoon, then forming a 'B' with your hand, as it's the first meal of the day.

Lunch: For 'lunch', use the L-handshape and mimic the motion of putting food into your mouth. It's the meal in the middle of the day, represented by the 'L'.

Dinner: Sign 'dinner' by using a flat handshape and moving it down from your mouth, representing the main meal that is often eaten in the evening.

Snacks: The sign for 'snacks' is similar to 'eat' but is often done with a more casual or repetitive gesture, indicating small, informal eating.

Eat: Mimic the action of bringing food to your mouth with your dominant hand. This sign is straightforward and universal for eating.

Drink: Pretend to hold a cup in your hand and tip it towards your mouth, mimicking the action of drinking.

Cook: Use a stirring motion, as if stirring a pot, to indicate 'cook'. This sign represents the general action of cooking food.

Bake: Mime placing a tray into an oven, indicating the specific action of baking.

Grill: Use a flipping motion, as if you are flipping food on a grill, to sign 'grill'.

Describing Tastes and Flavors

Sweet: The sign for 'sweet' involves moving your open hand in a small arc across your lips. Think of the gesture as mimicking the enjoyment of a sweet flavor on your tongue.

Salty: To indicate 'salty', pinch your fingers together and then shake them near your lips, as if sprinkling salt.

Spicy: The sign for 'spicy' is like fanning your mouth with your hand, indicating the sensation of eating something with a strong, hot flavor.

Bitter: For 'bitter', make a face that shows distaste (like a wrinkled nose) and flick your fingers away from your chin. This non-manual expression is crucial to convey the sense of bitterness.

Sour: To sign 'sour', make a puckered lip expression and twist your hand near your mouth, indicating a tangy or tart taste.

Discussing Dietary Preferences and Restrictions

ALLERGY

Allergies: To discuss allergies, use the sign for 'ALLERGY' which involves touching your cheek with the fingers and then flicking them away, followed by signing what you are allergic to, like 'NUTS', 'DAIRY', or 'EGGS'.

Vegetarian: The sign for 'vegetarian' involves forming a 'V' handshape with your fingers and then placing it near your mouth. It symbolizes a diet that primarily consists of vegetables.

Vegan: For 'vegan', use the same sign as 'vegetarian' but with more emphasis, or you can spell out 'V-E-G-A-N'. This distinction is important to convey the absence of all animal products.

Gluten-Free: To indicate 'gluten-free', you can spell out 'G-L-U-T-E-N' and then sign 'NO' or 'FREE'. This sign combination communicates the avoidance of gluten.

Lactose Intolerant: For lactose intolerance, you can sign 'MILK' followed by 'NO' or 'BAD', indicating an adverse reaction to dairy.

Lesson 14: Verbs in ASL

Understanding ASL Verb Structure

The structure of verbs in American Sign Language (ASL) is unique, with several key aspects differentiating it from spoken languages. Understanding these nuances is crucial for effective communication.

Directionality: Many ASL verbs are directional, meaning their movement or orientation changes to show who is doing what to whom. For example, the sign for 'ask' changes direction depending on who is asking whom.

Movement: The movement of a verb sign can convey information about the action's duration, intensity, or nature. For instance, a quick movement in the sign for 'run' can indicate running fast, while a slow movement can imply jogging.

Non-Manual Markers: Facial expressions, head movements, and body posture play a significant role in verb usage in ASL. They can indicate tense, mood, or modify the meaning of the verb. For example, furrowed brows can accompany a verb to indicate a question.

Verb Agreement: ASL uses subject-verb-object agreement in a visual-spatial way. The direction in which a verb sign moves can indicate the subject and object of the verb. This aspect is particularly important in ASL grammar.

Classifiers as Verbs: In ASL, classifiers are used to represent verbs. These are handshapes that represent objects or persons and show their movement or placement. For example, a classifier can be used to show a car driving down a street.

Compound Verbs: Some ASL verbs are compound, meaning they combine two concepts. For example, the sign for 'drive' might combine 'car' and 'go'.

Common Action Verbs

Go: Use a pointed index finger and move your hand forward. The movement represents the action of moving from one place to another.

GO

Come: With a pointed index finger, start with your hand away from your body and move it toward your chest. It indicates something or someone coming toward you.

See: Point to your eyes with two fingers and then point forward. The sign mimics the act of looking or seeing something.

Eat: Bring your hand to your mouth as if holding food, closing your fingers to your thumb. It resembles the action of putting food into your mouth.

Drink: Form a 'C' handshape and mimic the action of tilting a cup into your mouth. This sign represents the act of drinking a liquid.

Sleep: Place your hand flat against your face, palm down, and tilt your head onto it, closing your eyes. This sign imitates the posture of sleeping.

Read: Hold your non-dominant hand flat, representing a book, and move your dominant hand's index finger across it as if following text lines

Write: Pretend to hold a pen and move it across your non-dominant hand as if it's paper. This sign illustrates the act of writing.

Work: With fists, alternate upward movement as if hammering. This sign is a general representation of doing work or labor.

Play: Use a 'Y' handshape and shake it back and forth. This sign is often used to indicate playing, leisure, or fun activities.

Directional Verbs

Give: The sign for 'give' is made by extending your hands outward from your body. The direction you move your hands indicates who is giving to whom. For instance, moving hands from yourself to another direction means "I give to you".

Show: To sign 'show', hold your palm up and move it from the signer to the direction of the person being shown. The direction of the hand movement indicates who is showing something to whom.

Take: 'Take' is signed by moving your hand toward your body. The starting point and direction of the movement can indicate from whom you are taking something.

Send: To sign 'send', use a handshape as if you are pushing something away from your body towards another direction. The movement from one point to another indicates the sender and receiver.

Verb Agreement

Directional Verbs and Agreement: In ASL, many verbs are directional, meaning their motion indicates the subject and object. For example, the verb 'give' changes direction based on who is giving to whom. If you are signing 'I give to you', the motion is from the signer towards the direction of the person being addressed.

Agreement in Pronouns: Pronouns in ASL also agree with the verbs. For instance, the sign for 'help' will change direction depending on who is helping whom. If you are signing 'She helps him', the motion goes from the direction of the signer indicating 'she' to another direction indicating 'him'.

Pluralization: Verb agreement can also indicate plural subjects or objects. For example, a sweeping motion while signing 'see' can indicate seeing multiple people or things, rather than a single person or item.

Temporal Aspect and Agreement: The aspect of a verb (how the action occurs over time) can also be part of the agreement. For example, continuous aspect can be indicated by repeating the verb sign.

Non-Manual Markers and Verbs

Facial Expressions: Facial expressions can significantly change the meaning of a verb. For example, furrowing your brows while signing 'know' can turn it into a question, as in "Do you know?" Similarly, a look of surprise can add emphasis or intensity to a verb.

Head Movements: Nodding or shaking your head while signing can indicate agreement or negation, respectively. For instance, nodding while signing 'go' can affirm a decision to leave.

Body Posture: The orientation and movement of your body can also convey aspects of verbs. Leaning forward slightly can indicate future tense, while leaning back can indicate past tense.

Eye Gaze: The direction of your gaze can accompany verbs to indicate the direction of the action or the object of the verb. For example, looking towards the person you are speaking about while signing 'help' clarifies who is being helped.

Mouth Morphemes: Certain mouth shapes and movements can modify the meaning of verbs. For instance, a 'cha' mouth shape with a verb can indicate largeness or intensity.

Interactive Verb Games

ASL Verb Charades: In this game, participants take turns acting out a verb without speaking while others guess the verb being signed. This helps in recognizing and understanding various verb signs.

Storytelling Challenges: Create a game where each participant tells a story using ASL, focusing on incorporating as many verbs as possible. This can be done in a round-robin format, where each person adds to the story with a new verb

Verb Relay: In groups, have participants communicate a verb to the next person using only ASL. The last person in the line then guesses the verb. This game can be timed for added challenge.

Verb Pictionary: Similar to traditional Pictionary, but with verbs. Participants draw scenarios or actions depicting a verb, and others guess the verb being drawn.

Verb Bingo: Create bingo cards with different verbs. Call out actions or scenarios, and participants mark off the corresponding verb on their cards. The first to complete a line wins.

Verb Matching Game: Use cards with verbs and their definitions or illustrations. Participants match the verb sign to its correct meaning. This can also be played as a memory matching game.

Verb Guessing Game: One person signs a verb, and others ask yes/no questions to guess the verb. This game also reinforces the use of question signs in ASL.

Verb Simon Says: Play a version of Simon Says using ASL verbs. This helps participants practice both understanding and correctly executing verb signs.

Verb Construction Challenge: Give participants a set of verbs and challenge them to construct as many sentences as possible within a time limit.

ASL Verb Hangman: Play hangman using verbs. This game can reinforce the spelling and recognition of verbs in ASL.

Lesson 15: Most Common phrases

Greetings and Farewells

Being able to properly greet and bid farewell is a fundamental aspect of communication in American Sign Language (ASL). Here's how to sign some common greetings and farewells:

Hello: Simply wave your hand as you would in a typical greeting. This universal gesture is also used in ASL.

Good Morning: For 'good morning', sign 'good' by placing your open hand on your chin and moving it down to your other hand, followed by the sign for 'morning'. The morning sign is made by placing your arm horizontally, then moving your other hand up along it, like the sun rising.

Good Night: To say 'good night', first sign 'good', then 'night'. For 'night', hold your fingers flat and palm down, then flip them to palm up, representing the sun going down and the onset of night.

Goodbye: Just like 'hello', waving your hand is the common sign for 'goodbye' in ASL.

See You Later: For this, use the sign for 'see' by pointing your index finger to your eyes, then 'later' by hooking your index finger and thumb together and moving it away from your body.

Take Care: First, sign 'take' by mimicking the action of grabbing something with your hand, and then 'care' by interlocking your fingers and then moving your hands in a circular motion in front of your chest.

Basic Courtesies

Please: Place your flat hand on your chest and move it in a circular motion. This gesture is akin to a gentle request or plea.

Thank You: Similarly, start with your flat hand on your lips and move it forward. It's as if expressing gratitude that comes from within.

Sorry: Form a fist with your dominant hand and rub it in a circular motion over your heart. This sign symbolizes regret coming from the heart.

Excuse Me: Use a slight bow of your head with a respectful facial expression, and sign 'excuse' by twisting a '5' handshape in front of your body. It indicates a polite request for attention or forgiveness for an interruption.

Common Questions

How are you?: Start with the sign for 'how', which is done by placing both flat hands in front of you, palms facing up, and then shrugging your shoulders slightly. Follow this with the sign for 'you' by pointing at the person you're asking.

What's your name?: For 'what', open your hands, palms up, and shake them side to side a few times. Then sign 'your' by pointing towards the person you're asking, and finish with 'name' by using two fingers to tap on your other palm twice.

NAME

Where are you from?: Sign 'where' by holding your index finger up and shaking it side to side. Follow with 'you' and 'from', which is signed by pointing your index fingers toward each other and then moving them away in opposite directions.

Can you help me?: Start with the sign for 'can' by making a fist with your thumb sticking out on top, and then place it on your chest. Follow this with 'you' and 'help', which is signed by placing your fist in your palm and lifting it upwards, and then point towards yourself for 'me'.

Responses to Common Questions

I'm Fine, Thank You: To respond to 'How are you?', sign 'fine' by touching your thumb to your chest and then moving your hand outwards and slightly upwards. Follow this with 'thank you', as described previously.

My Name Is...: In response to 'What's your name?', sign 'my' by placing your flat hand on your chest. Then sign 'name' as previously described, followed by finger-spelling your name.

I'm from...: When asked 'Where are you from?', sign 'from' by pointing both index fingers towards each other and then moving them away. Follow this by finger-spelling the name of your city, state, or country.

Yes, I Can Help You: To respond to 'Can you help me?', sign 'yes' by nodding your head and making a fist with your thumb sticking up. Then sign 'I help you' by using the sign for 'help' and directing it towards the person you are speaking to.

Everyday Expressions

I Don't Understand: To sign 'I don't understand', shake your head to indicate 'no' or 'don't', and then point to your forehead. This gesture symbolizes a lack of comprehension or understanding.

Please Repeat: For 'please repeat', sign 'please' as previously mentioned, followed by 'repeat'. To sign 'repeat', use a circular motion with one hand, indicating the action of doing something again.

I Agree: To express agreement, simply nod your head and sign 'agree', which is done by forming two 'A' handshapes (fist with thumb beside the side of the fist) and moving them together in a small circular motion in front of you.

How Do You Sign...?: To ask how to sign a particular word, start with the sign for 'how', then point to the object or concept if present, or finger-spell the word, and finish with the sign for 'sign', which is done by pointing to your index finger of the non-dominant hand with the index finger of your dominant hand.

Expressing Needs and Wants

I Need Help: Sign 'need' by placing both fists together in front of you, with your dominant fist on top. Then sign 'help' by placing your closed fist in your open palm and lifting upwards. Combine these signs to express the need for assistance.

HELP

I Want to Learn: Start with the sign for 'want', which is made by extending your fingers and pulling them into your chest twice. Follow this with 'learn', signed by placing your dominant hand open, palm up, under your non-dominant hand and then lifting it up to your forehead.

I Would Like...: To express a polite desire, start with 'I would like', which is similar to 'want' but done in a more gentle manner. Then, indicate what you would like, either by signing the specific item or activity, or by finger-spelling it.

Common Mistakes and How to Avoid Them

Incorrect Handshapes or Movements: Mistakes often arise from incorrect handshapes or movements, which can change the meaning of a phrase. To avoid this, practice each phrase slowly and deliberately, focusing on the precision of your handshapes and movements. Regularly refer to reliable ASL resources or seek feedback from experienced ASL users.

Misinterpreting Non-Manual Markers: Non-manual markers like facial expressions and body language are crucial in ASL. An incorrect expression can alter the meaning of your phrase. Be conscious of your facial expressions and ensure they match the sentiment of what you're signing. Practice in front of a mirror or record yourself to self-evaluate.

Confusing Similar Phrases: Some phrases in ASL can look visually similar. For instance, 'I need help' and 'I want help' may be confused if not signed distinctly. Practice phrases that are similar side by side to understand their differences better.

Week IV: Communication skills improvement

Lesson 16: Medical and Emergency Signs

In critical situations, being able to communicate effectively in American Sign Language (ASL) can be life-saving. This chapter focuses on essential signs related to medical and emergency situations, helping learners to convey urgent information quickly and accurately.

Basic Medical Terms

Doctor: Form a 'D' handshape (index finger and thumb forming a circle, other fingers extended) and tap it on your wrist, where a doctor might wear a wristwatch.

DOCTOR

Hospital: Spell 'H' (two fingers extended and spread apart, thumb in between) and circle it in front of your shoulder, indicating a place of care.

Medicine: Pretend to be swallowing a pill or form a 'C' handshape and bring it to your mouth as if consuming medicine.

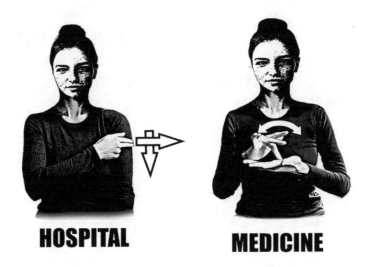

HOSPITAL   **MEDICINE**

Pain: Use your index fingers to point to the area where the pain is located. For general pain, you can also twist your index fingers near your temples.

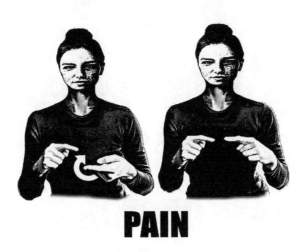

PAIN

Nurse: Make an 'N' handshape (thumb and little finger extended, other fingers tucked down) and tap it on one shoulder, then the other. This sign is similar to the sign for 'doctor' but uses the 'N' handshape.

Sick: Place your middle finger on your forehead and your thumb on your stomach, indicating feelings of illness or nausea.

SICK

Injury: Point to or indicate the area of injury. For a general sign, you can use an open hand to tap on your other arm, suggesting hurt or injury.

Emergency: Form 'E' handshapes with both hands (index finger extended, other fingers folded down) and rotate them at the sides of your head, suggesting urgency or a critical situation.

Describing Symptoms

Cover signs for describing common symptoms like 'fever', 'cough', 'headache', 'nausea', 'dizziness', and 'allergy'. This section helps in accurately conveying how you or someone else is feeling.

Emergency Situations

Fever: To indicate 'fever', touch your forehead with the back of your fingers, suggesting a temperature check. You can add a facial expression that shows discomfort to convey the feeling of fever.

Cough: Mimic the action of coughing by placing your hand in front of your mouth and making a slight coughing gesture. Ensure your facial expression matches the discomfort of coughing.

COUCH

Headache: To sign 'headache', use your fingers to show pain in specific areas of your head, like the temples or forehead. Squeeze your fingers slightly to indicate the pressure or pain of a headache.

Nausea: For 'nausea', place one hand near your stomach and the other near your mouth, with a facial expression that shows discomfort or sickness.

Dizziness: Indicate 'dizziness' by pointing to your head with a spinning motion and a disoriented facial expression. This sign mimics the feeling of unsteadiness or spinning.

Allergy: For 'allergy', use your index finger to tap on your nose or make a gesture that suggests sneezing or a reaction, depending on the specific allergy symptoms.

Instructions and Directions

Stay Calm: To convey 'stay calm', use a flat handshape, palms down, and move your hands gently down in a calming manner. Accompany this with a calm facial expression.

Call 911: First, sign 'call' by mimicking the use of a telephone with your hand. Then, finger-spell 9-1-1.

911

Exit: The sign for 'exit' involves pointing your thumb over your shoulder or towards the direction of the nearest exit. It's like showing the way out.

Safe: Indicate 'safe' by using both hands to form an 'S' handshape (fist with thumb over fingers) and then moving them down in front of the body, showing a sense of security or safety.

Where is the Nearest Hospital?: Start with the sign for 'where' (index finger moving side to side), then sign 'nearest' by bringing your hands together, and finally, sign 'hospital' as previously described.

Communicating with Healthcare Professionals

I Need a Doctor: To sign this, first sign 'I' by pointing to yourself, then 'need' by bringing your fists together in front of you, and finally 'doctor' using the 'D' handshape tapped on your wrist.

I Have an Appointment: Start with the sign for 'I', followed by 'have', which is signed by placing your hand on your chest. Then sign 'appointment' by circling your index finger and then pointing to your wrist, indicating a scheduled time.

What is the Treatment?: Begin with 'what', signed by holding your palms up and shaking them side to side. Continue with 'is' by pointing up with your index finger, and finish with 'treatment', which can be signed by showing a 'T' handshape and moving your hand in a small circular motion.

How Long Will It Take?: Sign 'how long' by holding your hands apart in front of you, palms facing each other, and moving them to indicate duration. Follow this with 'will', signed by moving your open hand forward, and 'take' by grabbing something with your hand and pulling it towards you.

Where Is the Pharmacy?: Sign 'where' with your index finger moving side to side. Then sign 'pharmacy' by spelling out 'P-H' (if there's no established sign), or use the common sign for 'medicine' followed by the sign for 'place'.

Lesson 17: ASL for Parents and Guardians

For parents and guardians, being able to communicate in American Sign Language (ASL) can be incredibly valuable, especially if their child is Deaf or hard of hearing. This chapter focuses on ASL signs and phrases crucial for everyday parenting and guardianship.

Basic Parenting Phrases

I Love You: This iconic sign is made by raising your pinky, index finger, and thumb, while keeping the other two fingers down. It combines the signs for the letters 'I', 'L', and 'Y' from 'I Love You'.

Time for Bed: For 'time', point to your wrist as if indicating a watch. Then sign 'for' by bringing both index fingers together, and 'bed' by placing your hands together at the side of your head, mimicking the act of resting your head on a pillow.

Eat Your Food: First, sign 'eat' by bringing your hand to your mouth as if holding food. Follow this with 'your', pointing towards the child, and then 'food', which is signed by miming the act of eating.

Be Careful: To sign 'be careful', form your hands into flat shapes and move them slowly and cautiously in a downward motion in front of your body, indicating the need for caution.

Do Your Homework: Start with 'do' by using a twisting motion with both fists in front of you. Then point towards the child for 'your', and finally, sign 'homework' by showing one hand in the shape of a 'flat O' and tapping it with the palm of your other hand, as if writing on it.

Encouraging and Comforting Signs

Good Job: To sign 'good', place your open hand on your chin and move it down to your other hand. Follow this with 'job', which can be signed by forming both hands into fists and tapping them together twice.

I'm Proud of You: Start with 'I' by pointing to yourself. For 'proud', puff up your chest and pat it with your fingers. Then point towards the child for 'you'. The sign for 'proud' is like showing a feeling swelling in your chest.

Don't Worry: Sign 'don't' by extending your index finger and moving it sideways in front of you, like cutting off further action. Then, sign 'worry' by twisting your hands back and forth in front of your forehead, indicating a troubled mind.

It's Okay: To convey 'it's okay', form a handshape like you're holding a plate in one hand, then brush it with the palm of your other hand. This sign is similar to reassuring someone that things are fine.

You Can Do It: Point to the child for 'you', sign 'can' by making a fist with your thumb sticking out on top and placing it on your chest, and then sign 'do it' by using a twisting motion with both fists in front of you, similar to turning knobs or handles.

Discipline and Rules

No: The sign for 'no' is straightforward – cross your index and middle fingers, resembling the common gesture for 'no' or 'not allowed'.

Stop: To sign 'stop', extend your dominant hand, palm facing outward, as if signaling someone to halt. This sign is firm and clear.

Listen to Me: Begin with the sign for 'listen' by placing your hand near your ear. Follow this with pointing to yourself for 'me'. It's important to have an assertive facial expression to convey the seriousness of the instruction.

Be Quiet: Sign 'be quiet' by placing your index finger over your lips. It's similar to the universal gesture for asking someone to be silent.

Wait Your Turn: For 'wait', wiggle your fingers while holding your hand up. Then sign 'your turn' by pointing to the child and then gesturing a turn-taking motion.

Communicating Needs and Requests

I'm Hungry: To express hunger, sign 'I'm' by pointing to yourself, and then sign 'hungry' by touching your chest with the fingertips of your dominant hand and moving them in a circular motion.

I'm Thirsty: Indicate thirst by signing 'I'm' followed by 'thirsty.' For 'thirsty,' form an 'X' with your index fingers and tap them together twice in front of your mouth.

I Need Help: To request assistance, sign 'I' by pointing to yourself, then sign 'need' by extending your open hand outward from your body. Finally, sign 'help' by forming an 'H' with your dominant hand and bringing it to your non-dominant hand.

Can We Play?: To ask if it's time to play, sign 'can' by forming a 'C' with your dominant hand and shaking it slightly. Follow this with 'we' and 'play' to complete the question.

Read Me a Story: Encourage storytelling by signing 'read' with your dominant hand holding an imaginary book and moving it as if reading. Then sign 'me' and 'story' sequentially.

Lesson 18: More important communication topics

Expressing Emotions and Feelings

Happy: To sign "happy," use both hands and make gentle, upward movements while smiling. It's important to convey the emotion through your facial expression.

Sad: Sign "sad" by moving your dominant hand downward from your non-dominant hand, mimicking a downward expression of sadness. Your facial expression should reflect the emotion.

Excited: Express excitement by signing "excited" with both hands in a "5" handshape near your chest and vibrating them outward while showing an enthusiastic facial expression.

Angry: Sign "angry" by forming claw-like "5" handshapes and bringing them toward your body in a forceful manner. Your facial expression should convey anger

Nervous: For "nervous," use the sign that resembles wringing your hands together, showing uneasiness. Your facial expression should reflect nervousness.

Surprised: Indicate surprise by opening your eyes wide, raising your eyebrows, and showing amazement on your face. You can use this expression for various surprised situations.

Confused: Sign "confused" by tapping your forehead with your index finger while wearing a puzzled expression. This signifies a state of confusion.

Proud: To convey "proud," use your dominant hand to pat your chest in an upward motion while wearing a proud facial expression.

Shy: Show shyness by tilting your head slightly down and glancing away while using a reserved expression.

Frustrated: Express "frustrated" by using both hands to mimic a sense of things falling apart. Your facial expression should convey frustration

Calm: Sign "calm" by placing your non-dominant hand near your chest and making a "C" shape with your dominant hand while wearing a relaxed facial expression.

In Love: Convey being "in love" by crossing your arms over your chest in an X shape, forming a heart, while showing affection on your face.

Embarrassed: Show embarrassment by gently touching your cheek with a closed hand while blushing or looking away.

Grateful: Express gratitude by forming the letter "G" with your dominant hand and moving it from your chin outward while smiling.

Lonely: Sign "lonely" by making a "U" shape with your index fingers and moving them apart while wearing a sad expression

Content: To indicate contentment, sign with your non-dominant hand near your chest and your dominant hand forming a "C" shape while showing a peaceful facial expression.

Describing Weather Conditions

Sunny: Sign "sunny" by using both hands to represent the sun's rays. Extend your fingers upward and outward from a central point on your non-dominant hand, resembling the sun's rays.

Rainy: To convey "rainy," mimic rain falling from the sky by using your fingers to create downward movements.

Snowy: Sign "snowy" by using your fingers to mimic falling snowflakes in the air.

Windy: For "windy," simulate the blowing wind by moving your flat hand in a back-and-forth motion, showing the direction of the wind.

Cloudy: Sign "cloudy" by forming both hands into "5" handshapes and bringing them together in front of you to represent clouds covering the sky.

Foggy: To express "foggy," make a sweeping motion in front of your face with an open hand to represent the dense fog.

Stormy: Sign "stormy" by using your dominant hand to mimic lightning bolts in the sky.

Hot: For "hot," fan your face with your hand as if you're trying to cool down due to the heat.

Cold: To indicate "cold," hug yourself and shiver slightly, simulating the feeling of cold temperatures.

Clear: Sign "clear" by using your non-dominant hand as a base and sweeping your dominant hand across the sky to represent clear, unobstructed conditions.

Partly Cloudy: Combine the signs for "part" and "cloudy" to indicate "partly cloudy." Use the "5" handshapes to represent clouds partially covering the sky.

Breezy: Sign "breezy" by making a waving motion with your flat hand to represent a gentle breeze.

Humid: To convey "humid," use your non-dominant hand as a base and bring your dominant hand forward while fanning yourself

Freezing: Indicate "freezing" by using your dominant hand to make a shivering motion.

Misty: Sign "misty" by simulating light rain or mist falling from the sky with your fingers.

Hail: To express "hail," make small, repetitive tapping motions with your fingertips.

Talking About Hobbies and Interests

Sports: To discuss sports, you can fingerspell the name of the sport you're interested in or use specific signs if they exist. For example, "basketball" can be fingerspelled, or you can use the sign for "basketball" if it's commonly recognized.

Music: Express your love for music by signing "music." Use both hands in a rhythmic tapping motion on your chest, representing the beat of the music.

Art: Sign "art" by forming both hands into "A" handshapes and moving them in a circular motion in front of your chest. This represents the act of creating art.

Reading: To convey "reading," use one hand to mimic flipping through the pages of a book.

Cooking: Sign "cooking" by pretending to stir a pot on an imaginary stove

Gardening: Show your interest in gardening by signing "garden." Use one hand to represent planting seeds or tending to plants.

Traveling: Indicate "traveling" by using both hands to mimic the motion of a plane taking off.

Photography: Express your love for photography by forming the letter "C" with one hand and using it to frame a shot in front of your eye.

Dancing: Sign "dance" by moving your body in a rhythmic and expressive manner, imitating dance movements.

Movies: To discuss movies, you can fingerspell the title of the movie or simply use the sign for "movie" by framing a rectangle with your fingers to represent a screen.

Hiking: Show your passion for hiking by using one hand to mimic walking on a trail.

Collecting: For "collecting," use one hand to show placing items into a collection, emphasizing the act of gathering.

Volunteering: Indicate "volunteering" by using your dominant hand to represent helping or giving while your non-dominant hand represents receiving.

Fitness: Sign "fitness" by forming an "F" handshape and moving it up and down in front of your body, representing exercise.

Animals/Pets: Express your love for animals or pets by fingerspelling the name of the animal or using specific signs if they exist. For example, "dog" can be fingerspelled, or you can use the sign for "dog."

Crafts: Sign "crafts" by using one hand to represent crafting activities like knitting, sewing, or crafting with paper.

Video Games: To discuss video games, you can fingerspell the title of the game or use the sign for "video game" by mimicking holding a game controller.

Discussing Technology and Gadgets

Computer: Sign "computer" by forming the letter "C" with both hands and mimicking typing on a keyboard.

Smartphone: Indicate "smartphone" by forming a "phone" sign with one hand and tapping your thumb and index finger on an imaginary screen.

Tablet: Sign "tablet" by mimicking holding a tablet with both hands and tapping the screen.

Internet: To discuss the "internet," use both hands to mimic the shape of the Earth and move them in a circular motion, symbolizing the global network.

Website: Sign "website" by forming the letter "W" with one hand and tracing it in the air to represent a webpage.

Email: Express "email" by forming the letter "E" with one hand and mimicking the motion of typing an email.

Social Media: To discuss "social media," use both hands to sign "S" (the first letter of "social") and then gesture to represent a feed or timeline.

Search: Sign "search" by forming the letter "S" with one hand and moving it in a searching motion in front of you.

App: To indicate an "app" or application, use one hand to mimic tapping on a smartphone screen.

Wi-Fi: Sign "Wi-Fi" by forming the letter "W" with one hand and moving it in a circular motion, representing a wireless signal.

Password: Express "password" by forming the letter "P" with one hand and mimicking typing a password on a keyboard.

Download: Sign "download" by forming the letter "D" with one hand and moving it downward, symbolizing the transfer of data.

Upload: To discuss "upload," use one hand to form the letter "U" and move it upward to represent sending data.

Bluetooth: Sign "Bluetooth" by forming a "B" with one hand and moving it toward your ear, symbolizing wireless connectivity.

GPS: Indicate "GPS" by forming a "G" with one hand and mimicking the screen of a GPS device.

Camera: To discuss a "camera," form the letter "C" with both hands and mimic holding a camera to take a photo.

Virtual Reality: Express "virtual reality" by forming the letter "V" with both hands and creating a visual representation of a virtual world around your head.

Streaming: Sign "streaming" by forming an "S" with one hand and making a forward motion, symbolizing the flow of content.

Transportation and Travel

Car: Sign "car" by mimicking holding a steering wheel with both hands and driving.

Bus: Express "bus" by forming the letter "B" with one hand and moving it forward, simulating a bus moving along a road.

Train: Sign "train" by forming the letter "T" with one hand and moving it along an imaginary train track.

TRAIN

Subway: To discuss the "subway," use one hand to mimic holding onto a subway pole while the other hand forms the letter "S."

Bicycle: Sign "bicycle" by mimicking pedaling a bike with both hands.

Motorcycle: Express "motorcycle" by forming the letter "M" with one hand and mimicking the grip of motorcycle handlebars.

Airplane: Sign "airplane" by forming the letter "A" with one hand and mimicking the wings of an airplane.

Boat: To discuss a "boat," form the letter "B" with one hand and move it in a wave-like motion.

Walk: Sign "walk" by mimicking the act of walking with two fingers of one hand.

Run: Express "run" by mimicking running in place with two fingers of one hand.

Ticket: Sign "ticket" by forming the letter "T" with one hand and mimicking handing over a ticket.

TICKET

Drive: To indicate "drive," mime holding a steering wheel with both hands and turning it.

Fly: Sign "fly" by forming the letter "F" with one hand and making a flying motion.

Sail: Express "sail" by forming the letter "S" with one hand and moving it forward, symbolizing a sailboat sailing.

Luggage: To discuss "luggage," use both hands to mime holding and carrying a suitcase.

Airport: Sign "airport" by forming the letter "A" with one hand and mimicking the shape of an airport terminal.

Hotel: Express "hotel" by forming the letter "H" with one hand and indicating a building's shape.

Destination: Sign "destination" by forming the letter "D" with one hand and pointing in the direction of your destination.

Travel: To talk about "travel," form the letter "T" with one hand and make a forward motion.

Vacation: Sign "vacation" by forming the letter "V" with one hand and mimicking relaxing on a beach.

Social Media and Online Communication

Social Media: Sign "social media" by forming the letter "S" with one hand and making a circular motion, symbolizing the interconnectedness of social networks.

Facebook: Express "Facebook" by forming an "F" with one hand and mimicking scrolling through a Facebook feed.

Twitter: Sign "Twitter" by forming a "T" with one hand and mimicking typing on a keyboard, representing tweeting.

Instagram: To discuss "Instagram," form an "I" with one hand and mimic scrolling through

Snapchat: Sign "Snapchat" by forming an "S" with one hand and mimicking the act of sending a snap.

YouTube: Express "YouTube" by forming a "Y" with one hand and mimicking the play button on a video.

TikTok: Sign "TikTok" by forming a "T" with one hand and mimicking the swiping motion used in the app.

Hashtag: To talk about a "hashtag," form a "H" with one hand and use the other hand to mimic typing a hashtag symbol.

Like: Sign "like" by making a thumbs-up gesture.

Comment: Express "comment" by forming a "C" with one hand and mimicking typing on a keyboard.

Share: To discuss "share," mime holding an imaginary post and moving it to someone else.

Follow: Sign "follow" by forming an "F" with one hand and making a forward motion, indicating following someone's updates.

Message: Express "message" by forming an "M" with one hand and mimicking the act of sending a message.

Friend Request: To talk about a "friend request," mime sending and accepting a friend request.

Notification: Sign "notification" by forming an "N" with one hand and mimicking the act of receiving a notification.

Online: Express "online" by forming an "O" with one hand and indicating a computer screen.

Emoji: Sign "emoji" by forming an "E" with one hand and mimicking the act of sending an emoji.

Viral: To discuss something going "viral," mime the spreading motion of a virus with both hands

Streaming: Express "streaming" by forming an "S" with one hand and mimicking the act of streaming content.

Influencer: Sign "influencer" by forming an "I" with one hand and mimicking someone influencing others.

Shopping and Commerce

Store: Sign "store" by mimicking opening and closing doors with both hands, symbolizing a physical store's entrance.

Shop: Express "shop" by forming an "S" with one hand and mimicking the act of shopping.

Buy: Sign "buy" by forming a "B" with one hand and moving it towards your body, indicating purchasing something.

Sell: To discuss "sell," form an "S" with one hand and move it away from your body, indicating the selling action.

Money: Sign "money" by forming an "M" with one hand and rubbing your fingers together, representing cash

Credit Card: Express "credit card" by mimicking swiping a card through a card reader.

Cash Register: Sign "cash register" by forming a "C" with one hand and mimicking pressing buttons on a cash register.

Receipt: To talk about a "receipt," mime the action of receiving a receipt from a cashier.

Shopping Cart: Sign "shopping cart" by mimicking pushing a shopping cart.

Groceries: Express "groceries" by forming a "G" with one hand and mimicking carrying bags of groceries.

Clothing: Sign "clothing" by touching your fingers to your chest, indicating wearing clothes.

Shoes: To discuss "shoes," mime tying shoelaces or putting on shoes.

Size: Sign "size" by forming an "S" with one hand and indicating a specific size with the other hand.

Price: Express "price" by forming a "P" with one hand and signing the number to represent the cost.

Discount: To talk about a "discount," form a "D" with one hand and mimic lowering a price.

Sale: Sign "sale" by forming an "S" with one hand and shaking it gently to indicate a sale event.

Checkout: Express "checkout" by forming a "C" with one hand and mimicking the act of checking out at a cashier.

Bag: Sign "bag" by mimicking putting items into a bag.

Online Shopping: To discuss "online shopping," mime typing on a keyboard or using a smartphone.

Shopping List: Sign "shopping list" by mimicking writing a list with one hand and holding it with the other.

Discussing Current Events and News

News: Sign "news" by mimicking holding a newspaper with both hands and opening it.

Television: Express "television" by forming a "T" with one hand

and pretending to adjust the TV's knobs.

Radio: Sign "radio" by mimicking turning the dial on an old-fashioned radio.

Broadcast: To discuss a "broadcast," form a "B" with one hand and mimic speaking into a microphone.

Journalist/Reporter: Sign "journalist" or "reporter" by forming a "J" with one hand and moving it near your mouth to signify speaking

Interview: Express "interview" by mimicking two people having a conversation, one asking questions and the other answering.

Breaking News: Sign "breaking news" by forming a "B" with one hand and shaking it gently to indicate something significant happening.

Headlines: To discuss "headlines," point to your forehead with one hand, indicating the top news stories.

Politics: Sign "politics" by forming a "P" with one hand and moving it in a circular motion near your temple, indicating the political world.

Economy: Express "economy" by forming an "E" with one hand and moving it in a circular motion near your chest, representing financial matters.

Weather Forecast: Sign "weather forecast" by mimicking a weather reporter on TV.

Discussion/Debate: To talk about a "discussion" or "debate," mime a conversation between two people.

Opinion: Sign "opinion" by forming an "O" with one hand and touching your temple to indicate personal views.

World News: Express "world news" by forming a "W" with one hand and moving it in a circular motion to represent global news.

Local News: Sign "local news" by forming an "L" with one hand and moving it in a circular motion to signify news from your area.

Internet News: To discuss "internet news," mime typing on a keyboard or using a smartphone.

Social Media: Express "social media" by forming an "S" with one hand and mimicking scrolling through a social media feed.

Comment: Sign "comment" by forming a "C" with one hand and pretending to write a comment.

Share: To talk about "sharing" news, mime clicking a "share" button on a social media platform.

Awareness: Sign "awareness" by forming an "A" with one hand and touching your forehead to indicate being informed.

Emergencies and Safety

Emergency: Sign "emergency" by making the letter "E" with one hand and shaking it slightly in the air.

Help: To request "help," extend one hand outward, palm up, and make a lifting motion with your fingers.

Fire: Sign "fire" by mimicking the flickering flames with both hands.

Police: Express "police" by forming a "P" with one hand and moving it near your shoulder as if indicating a badge.

Ambulance: Sign "ambulance" by forming an "A" with one hand and mimicking the flashing lights on top of an ambulance.

Hospital: To discuss a "hospital," form an "H" with one hand and place it on your cheek to indicate a building.

Doctor: Express "doctor" by forming a "D" with one hand and moving it near your mouth as if mimicking a stethoscope.

Nurse: Sign "nurse" by forming an "N" with one hand and mimicking a nurse's cap.

Injury: To describe an "injury," point to the affected area of your body.

Safety: Sign "safety" by forming an "S" with one hand and moving it near your chest.

Danger: Express "danger" by forming both hands into "D" shapes and crossing them to signify a hazard.

Evacuate: To indicate "evacuation," make the letter "E" with one hand and move it away from your body.

Exit: Sign "exit" by pointing in the direction of the nearest exit.

Stay Calm: Form an "S" with one hand and place it near your heart to signify staying calm.

Rescue: To discuss "rescue," mimic lifting someone with both arms.

First Aid: Express "first aid" by forming an "F" with one hand and mimicking bandaging a wound.

Shelter: Sign "shelter" by forming an "S" with one hand and making a roof-like gesture.

Safety Drill: Mime conducting a safety drill.

Emergency Kit: Sign "emergency kit" by forming an "E" with one hand and indicating a bag.

Flashlight: Express "flashlight" by mimicking holding and turning on a flashlight.

Battery: Sign "battery" by forming a "B" with one hand and indicating a battery.

Water: To request "water," mime drinking from a cup.

Food: Express "food" by mimicking eating with your hand.

Blanket: Sign "blanket" by indicating wrapping a blanket around yourself.

Alert: Express "alert" by making a sudden, sharp motion with one hand.

Safe: Sign "safe" by forming an "S" with one hand and touching your forehead.

Emergency Contact: Mimic dialing a phone and express "emergency contact" with your hand.

CPR (Cardiopulmonary Resuscitation): Mime performing CPR.

Lesson 19: Expansion Techniques

Repetition: Repeating a sign or movement can emphasize the intensity or frequency of an action. For example, signing "EAT" with repeated movements can convey eating enthusiastically.

Role-Shifting: ASL often involves role-shifting, where a signer uses specific signs or facial expressions to represent different characters in a story or conversation. Role-shifting helps distinguish between who is doing what in a narrative.

Classifier Predicates: Classifiers are handshapes that represent categories of objects or people. They are used to provide more detail in descriptions or narratives. For instance, a "3-handshape" can represent a group of people.

Non-Manual Markers: Facial expressions, head movements, and body language play a crucial role in ASL. Non-manual markers can change the meaning of a sign or sentence. For example, raising your eyebrows while signing a question indicates that it's a question.

Spatial Agreement: ASL uses spatial relationships to indicate connections between objects or people. By placing signs in specific locations in signing space, you can clarify relationships and convey complex ideas.

Temporal Aspect: ASL can express the timing of events by incorporating specific signs or movements to indicate past, present, or future actions. Timing is an important aspect of storytelling and conveying when events occurred.

Size and Shape Specifiers: When describing objects, using size and shape specifiers helps convey specific details. For instance, signing "BIG" before signing an object's name indicates that it's large.

Directionality: Movement direction matters in ASL. By changing the direction of a sign, you can indicate the movement or direction of an action. For example, signing "CAR" while moving your hands forward conveys the idea of driving a car.

Number Incorporation: ASL allows for the incorporation of numbers into signs. This is useful for specifying quantities or counting items.

Facial Expressions: Facial expressions can convey emotions, attitudes, and nuances of meaning. They are an integral part of ASL and add depth to communication.

Sequential Sign Placement: When telling a story or describing a process, signs are placed in chronological order in signing space. This helps the viewer follow the sequence of events.

Conditional Statements: ASL can express conditional statements, such as "if...then..." constructions. These are used to convey hypothetical situations or cause-and-effect relationships.

Expansion of Time: ASL can expand or condense time to convey more information efficiently. This is particularly useful in storytelling or explaining events.

Simultaneous Information: ASL can convey multiple pieces of information simultaneously. For example, you can sign "I HAVE TWO CATS" by using one handshape to represent "CAT" and another handshape to indicate the number "TWO."

Depicting Verbs: ASL can depict actions and movements by using signs that visually represent the action itself. This is common in storytelling and describing events.

Lesson 20: Top Digital Resources for Learning ASL

In today's digital age, there is a wealth of online resources available to help individuals learn American Sign Language (ASL). Whether you're a beginner looking to get started or an intermediate learner seeking to improve your skills, these digital resources can be valuable tools on your ASL learning journey. Here are some of the top digital resources for learning ASL:

Websites and Online Courses

ASL University (Lifeprint): Lifeprint offers a comprehensive online ASL curriculum with lessons, videos, and quizzes.

Start ASL: Start ASL provides a range of free and paid courses, including ASL 1, 2, and 3, as well as specialized courses.

SignSchool: SignSchool offers interactive lessons, quizzes, and games for learning ASL at your own pace.

ASL Video Dictionaries

ASL Pro: ASL Pro is an extensive video dictionary featuring thousands of ASL signs, organized alphabetically.

ASL Deafined: ASL Deafined offers an online video dictionary and interactive lessons for learning ASL signs.

YouTube Channels

Bill Vicars (ASL University): Bill Vicars' YouTube channel features video lessons covering various ASL topics and vocabulary.

Mobile Apps

The ASL App: This app offers an ASL dictionary, lessons, and quizzes for iOS and Android devices.

SignSchool: SignSchool's mobile app provides on-the-go access to ASL lessons and games.

ASL Communities and Forums

ASL Reddit: The ASL subreddit is a community of ASL learners and signers who share resources, ask questions, and practice together.

ASL-STEM Forum: This forum focuses on ASL in science, technology, engineering, and mathematics fields.

Online ASL Dictionaries

Handspeak: Handspeak is an online ASL dictionary with thousands of signs, including variations and regional signs.

Signing Savvy: Signing Savvy offers a searchable ASL dictionary and learning resources.

Social Media Groups

Facebook ASL Groups: There are many Facebook groups dedicated to ASL learning and practice, such as "ASL Learning Community" and "ASL Practice Pals."

ASL Games and Quizzes

ASLPro.com Games: ASLPro.com offers interactive ASL games and quizzes to reinforce your learning.

ASLized!: ASLized! provides ASL quizzes and interactive activities for learners.

Video Streaming Services

Netflix and Amazon Prime Video: These streaming platforms offer ASL-interpreted content, including movies and TV shows, which can help improve comprehension.

Educational Platforms

Coursera and edX: These platforms offer ASL courses from universities and institutions for more structured learning.

Deaf Culture Websites

National Association of the Deaf (NAD): NAD's website provides resources on Deaf culture, advocacy, and ASL.

Deaf Linx: Deaf Linx offers a directory of Deaf-related websites and resources.

ASL Literature and Stories

Deaf Missions: Deaf Missions produces Christian content in ASL, including Bible stories and lessons.

ASL Storytelling on YouTube: Many signers on YouTube share ASL stories and narratives.

Podcasts

ASL Nook Podcast: ASL Nook offers a podcast with discussions on ASL grammar, Deaf culture, and more.

Interpreter Training Resources

Registry of Interpreters for the Deaf (RID): RID's website provides resources for aspiring ASL interpreters.

Online ASL Challenges:

ASL That!: ASL That! offers monthly ASL challenges to practice signing and expand vocabulary.

When using digital resources to learn ASL, it's essential to combine them with real-life practice and interaction with Deaf individuals and the Deaf community. Learning ASL is not only about mastering signs but also understanding Deaf culture and using ASL in meaningful contexts. Explore these resources, find what works best for your learning style, and enjoy your journey to becoming proficient in ASL.

Bonus: Bilingualism - ASL and English

Bilingualism in American Sign Language (ASL) and English is not just about knowing two languages; it's about navigating two distinct cultures and modes of communication. This chapter aims to provide strategies and insights for effectively switching between ASL and English, understanding the cultural nuances, and appreciating the linguistic richness of both languages.

Section 1: Understanding Bilingualism in ASL and English

Bilingualism in ASL and English presents a unique intersection of linguistic and cultural dynamics. This section delves into the core aspects of this bilingual landscape, exploring the distinct characteristics of both languages and their interplay.

The Linguistic Landscape

The journey begins with acknowledging the foundational differences between ASL and English. ASL, a visual-spatial language, communicates through signs made by hand movements, facial expressions, and body postures. In contrast, English, an auditory-verbal language, relies on spoken sounds and written words. This fundamental difference in modality shapes the way information is processed and communicated in each language, affecting everything from grammar to expression.

Grammatical Distinctions

One of the most prominent differences is in sentence structuring. English follows a linear syntax, typically adhering to a Subject-Verb-Object order. ASL, however, often uses a topic-comment structure, where the subject or topic is introduced first, followed by additional information or comment. Time concepts in ASL are also distinct, often conveyed through spatial references and non-manual markers, rather than the tense forms used in English. Understanding these differences is crucial for effective bilingual communication.

Vocabulary and Expressions

While there is some overlap in vocabulary, many ASL signs have no direct English equivalent, and vice versa. This difference is especially pronounced in idiomatic expressions and slang, where cultural context plays a significant role. Learning these aspects of ASL and English not only enhances language proficiency but also deepens cultural understanding.

Code-Switching

Navigating between ASL and English involves code-switching, a common practice among bilinguals. It's not just about translating words but adapting to different cultural and linguistic contexts. In educational settings, professional environments, or social gatherings, bilinguals might switch languages to accommodate the communication needs of their audience or express different aspects of their identity.

Communication Strategies

Effective bilingual communication goes beyond mere fluency in ASL and English. It involves understanding the nuances and subtleties of each language. For instance, translating English text into ASL requires an understanding of ASL's visual nature, using spatial structuring and facial expressions to convey meaning. Similarly, when translating ASL to English, it's important to capture the essence of the message rather than attempting a word-for-word translation.

Cultural Context

The final piece in understanding bilingualism in ASL and English lies in recognizing the cultural contexts that shape language use. Each language is embedded in its own cultural framework, influencing not just what is communicated but how it is done. Respect for these cultural differences is key to effective and meaningful bilingual communication.

Section 2: Language Acquisition and Learning Techniques

In the realm of bilingualism, especially in ASL and English, the journey of acquiring language skills is both fascinating and complex. This section delves into the nuances of this process, catering to both children and adult learners.

Language Development in Children

Children immersed in bilingual environments often display a unique trajectory in language acquisition. The process of learning ASL and English simultaneously fosters cognitive benefits like enhanced problem-solving skills and better adaptability to varying communication contexts. Early exposure to both languages can lead to a more profound understanding and appreciation of both Deaf and hearing cultures. This early bilingualism also enhances metalinguistic awareness, allowing children to understand and manipulate language structures with greater ease. Contrary to some beliefs, bilingual development does not confuse children. Instead, it enriches their communicative repertoire and cultural understanding.

Effective Learning Strategies for Adults

Adult learners face distinct challenges in acquiring a new language. Unlike children, adults often rely on more structured learning and benefit greatly from explicit grammar instruction and practical usage. Key strategies include immersion through interaction with native signers and engaging in English-speaking settings. Regular practice, consistency, and persistence are vital, as is the willingness to make and learn from mistakes. Utilizing technology, such as language learning apps and online resources, can provide flexible and interactive opportunities for adults to practice both ASL and English. Additionally, joining language learning groups or finding a language exchange partner can be immensely beneficial in providing real-life practice and cultural insights.

The Role of Technology in Language Learning

In today's digital age, technology plays a significant role in language acquisition. For ASL learners, video platforms are invaluable for observing and practicing sign language. Apps that provide ASL lessons and dictionaries help in building vocabulary and understanding nuances. For English, numerous online courses, apps, and platforms cater to various proficiency levels, offering interactive and engaging content. Virtual reality (VR) and augmented reality (AR) technologies are also emerging as powerful tools, providing immersive language learning experiences that mimic real-life interactions.

Cultural Immersion and Language Acquisition

Understanding and participating in the cultures associated with both ASL and English are crucial for language acquisition. Cultural immersion deepens linguistic skills and provides context to the language used. Participating in Deaf community events, attending ASL poetry slams, or engaging in English book clubs can offer rich, immersive experiences. Such participation not only enhances language skills but also provides a deeper understanding of the values, norms, and practices of each community. It's through these cultural experiences that language learners gain more than just communicative skills; they gain a gateway to the heart of each community's identity.

Section 3: Navigating Bilingual Environments

In the context of ASL and English bilingualism, navigating diverse environments requires a deep understanding of both languages and their associated cultures. This section explores how individuals proficient in both ASL and English can effectively operate in various settings, such as classrooms, workplaces, and social gatherings.

Classroom Dynamics

For educators and students in bilingual educational settings, the challenge is to ensure effective communication and inclusivity. Teachers proficient in both ASL and English have the unique opportunity to bridge the gap between Deaf and hearing students. Techniques like simultaneous communication (signing while speaking) can be employed, although it's important to be mindful of the limitations and potential misunderstandings this method might entail. Creating a classroom culture where both languages are valued equally encourages an environment of mutual respect and learning.

Professional Interactions

In the workplace, bilingualism in ASL and English can enhance communication and collaboration. For instance, in meetings, having a fluent ASL interpreter can ensure that Deaf employees are fully included. Understanding the nuances of both languages is crucial for conveying precise information and maintaining professional etiquette. Additionally, awareness of cultural norms in Deaf and hearing cultures can aid in navigating workplace dynamics more effectively.

Social Settings

Social interactions present a different set of challenges and opportunities for bilingual individuals. In environments where both Deaf and hearing individuals are present, the choice of language can impact inclusivity and participation. Being adept in both ASL and English allows for smoother interaction, facilitating a bridge between different communication styles. It's also an opportunity to educate others about Deaf culture and the significance of ASL, promoting greater understanding and acceptance.

Bilingual Communication Tools

Technology plays a vital role in facilitating bilingual communication. Video relay services (VRS) and video remote interpreting (VRI) services are essential tools that provide access to communication for Deaf individuals in predominantly English-speaking environments. Additionally, text-based communication tools can serve as a common ground, particularly in digital communications.

Cultural Competence

A significant aspect of navigating bilingual environments is cultural competence. Understanding the expectations, norms, and values of both Deaf and hearing cultures is essential. This understanding helps in avoiding cultural faux pas and fosters a sense of respect and inclusivity. Engaging with the community, participating in cultural events, and continuous learning about cultural norms are ways to develop and maintain this competence.

Adapting to Diverse Environments

Flexibility and adaptability are key in bilingual settings. Being able to gauge the language preferences of individuals in a given context and adjust accordingly is a valuable skill. It involves not only linguistic ability but also cultural sensitivity and situational awareness.

Embracing bilingualism in ASL and English opens doors to diverse experiences and deeper connections in both the Deaf and hearing worlds. This bonus chapter aims to empower learners with the knowledge and tools to navigate these two rich languages and cultures with ease and confidence.

Conclusion

Congratulations on completing your journey through this book on American Sign Language (ASL)! You've embarked on a path to understanding and communicating in one of the most expressive and vibrant languages in the world. As you wrap up your exploration of ASL, let's reflect on your achievements and look ahead to the possibilities that await you.

1. Celebrating Your Progress: Take a moment to celebrate how far you've come. You've learned the fundamentals of ASL, from the manual alphabet to sentence structure, and explored essential topics like family, food, and everyday communication. Your dedication to learning ASL is a commendable achievement in itself.

2. Embracing Cultural Awareness: Beyond the signs and gestures, you've gained insights into Deaf culture, which is an integral part of ASL. Understanding the values, traditions, and experiences of the Deaf community enriches your ability to communicate effectively and respectfully.

3. Continued Learning: Learning a language is a lifelong journey. ASL is no exception. There's always more to discover and explore, whether it's mastering advanced signs, deepening your understanding of Deaf culture, or honing your signing skills.

4. Building Connections: ASL opens doors to meaningful connections with Deaf individuals and the broader Deaf community. By using ASL, you can foster relationships, bridge communication gaps, and contribute to a more inclusive society.

5. Empowering Communication: ASL is a powerful tool for communication. Whether you plan to use it personally, professionally, or as a means of advocacy, your ability to sign in ASL can make a significant impact on others' lives.

6. Encouraging Others: Share your knowledge and passion for ASL with others. Encourage friends, family, and colleagues to embark on their own ASL learning journeys. Your enthusiasm can inspire and create a ripple effect of understanding and inclusion.

7. Nurturing Curiosity: Stay curious and open to new experiences. ASL is a dynamic language that evolves with time. Embrace opportunities to learn regional variations, slang, and emerging signs.

8. Lifelong Learning: Consider pursuing advanced studies in ASL, becoming a certified ASL interpreter, or exploring related fields such as Deaf education. Your expertise in ASL can open doors to diverse career paths.

9. Supporting the Deaf Community: Advocate for the rights and needs of the Deaf community. Promote accessibility, inclusivity, and equal opportunities for Deaf individuals in all aspects of life.

10. Your ASL Journey Continues: As you conclude this book, remember that your ASL journey is ongoing. Every conversation, every interaction, and every sign you learn contributes to your growth as a signer and a communicator. Embrace the beauty of ASL, its rich history, and its vibrant present.

Thank you for joining us on this ASL adventure. Your commitment to learning and embracing ASL enriches not only your life but also the lives of those with whom you communicate. Keep signing, keep learning, and keep sharing the gift of ASL with the world. Your journey has just

Made in the USA
Las Vegas, NV
06 February 2024

85330914R00072